SRA Reading Mastery®

Transformations

Reading

Textbook C

Siegfried Engelmann

Owen Engelmann

Karen Davis

McGraw Hill

Acknowledgments

The authors are grateful to the following people for their assistance in the preparations of Reading Mastery Transformations Grade 1 Reading.

Joanna Jachowicz
Blake Engelmann
Charlene Tolles-Engelmann
Cally Dwyer
Melissa Morrow
Toni Reeves

Emily Jachowicz for her valuable student input

We'd also like to acknowledge, from McGraw Hill, the valuable contributions by:

Mary Eisele
Nancy Stigers
Jason Yanok

mheducation.com/prek-12

Send all inquiries to:
McGraw-Hill Education
8787 Orion Place
Columbus, OH 43240

ISBN: 978-0-07-905408-1
MHID: 0-07-905408-0

Printed in the United States of America.

3 4 5 6 7 8 9 LWI 24 23 22 21

1. bay
2. held
3. winds
4. slept
5. honks

1. <u>act</u>ed
2. <u>clapp</u>ing
3. <u>blow</u>s
4. <u>give</u>s
5. <u>trip</u>s

1. crash
2. lash
3. dive
4. alive
5. lights
6. sights

1. o'clock
2. school
3. mind
4. parents

1. <u>sting</u>s
2. s<u>pot</u>s
3. un<u>less</u>
4. con<u>test</u>s
5. kn<u>own</u>
6. <u>tugg</u>ing

Donna
Part Three

The boy just before Donna was on the stage. He had a very short verse. He said, "I have a dog that is old. Her nose is always cold. I have a cat that is white. You can see him at night. Thank you." Everybody clapped.

Now it was Donna's turn. She walked out onto the stage. The lights were so bright that she could not see anybody in the crowd, but she could hear them. She said, "My verse is called 'The Sea.' It is made up by me."

Donna's hands were shaking as she held up her verse. But she tried to do what her mom told her to do. Here is what Donna said.

The winds they lash,
And the waves they crash.
Oh, how those waves roll and fall.
And there I am, alone and small.

Under those clouds, so white and high,
Where rock and sea meet sun and sky,
And the air is alive,
With birds that dive,
A sharp wind blows and gives sand wings,
And so it flies, and so it stings.
The sounds and sights feed my mind
With all the things I must leave behind.
So when I go, I take with me
The birds, the clouds, the wind, and the sea.

For a little while, the crowd was quiet. Then everybody started to clap and shout. Parents were standing and clapping.

Donna won the contest. "Thank you so much," she said. She had tears in her eyes.

Later that evening, she was telling her mom and dad how she felt when she was on stage. She said, "After I started to read my verse, I felt fine. But I was very scared before I started."

Her dad said, "Do you know that you are not speaking in verse now?"

Donna thought about what she had just said. Her dad was right. Donna said, "I can't believe it. I can talk like everybody else. This is wonderful."

And from that night on, Donna never talked in verse unless she wanted to. But she made up many verses. She won many contests, and she became very well known for her work.

The end.

1. live
2. live
3. read
4. read
5. dove
6. dove

cup   clam

1. On line 1, write about what the plate is under.

2. On line 2, write about what is under the fish.

Jan had to clean up all the feathers from the goose barn. There were a lot of feathers on the floor. Jan got a big broom and some bags to put the feathers in. Jan swept and swept. Soon she had all the feathers in a big pile near the door. Jan said, "Now that I am almost done, I will go outside and play." And she did. But when Jan opened the door to go out of the goose barn, the wind sent the pile of feathers all over the floor.

Later, Jan went back inside to put the pile of feathers in the bag. The goose barn was a mess. "What happened to my pile?" Jan yelled.

Jan had to do her job all over again. She was not very happy, but from now on, she won't play until her jobs are done.

1. What did Jan have to clean up in the goose barn?

2. After Jan swept the feathers in a big pile, she went outside to ▒▒▒▒ .

3. What sent the feathers all over the floor?

4. From now on, Jan won't play until her ▒▒▒▒▒▒ .

Star:

1. <u>barges</u>
2. <u>smashes</u>
3. <u>sleekest</u>
4. <u>ramming</u>
5. <u>puffed</u>
6. <u>crashing</u>

Moon:

1. m<u>ou</u>nt
2. motor
3. motorboat
4. bay
5. horn
6. tug

Clover:

1. <u>Tubby</u>
2. <u>smokey</u>
3. <u>dumpy</u>
4. <u>slow</u>ed
5. <u>fol</u>ded
6. <u>toast</u>ed

Heart:

1. pe<u>o</u>ple
2. phon<u>e</u>
3. phew
4. o'clock
5. stronger
6. school

A Trip to the Lake

Bob went with some friends on a field trip. Bob's mom dropped off Bob and his friends at a lake. She told them, "I'll come back and pick you up right here at three o'clock. Don't be late."

Bob's pals went looking for stones. Bob started looking at the toads that were near the lake. Then Bob walked over one hill and another hill. Soon, Bob did not know where he was. He was in a field with some goats. He said to himself, "How can I find my way back to the lake?"

One of the goats in the field was Gorman. He heard Bob talking to himself and said, "You are not a very large moose, but I can show you how to get back to the lake."

Bob tried to tell Gorman, "I am not a moose," but Gorman did not seem to listen.

Gorman led Bob around the hills.

Gorman could not see where he was going, and he didn't know where he was. But he acted as if he was leading Bob to the lake. He really led Bob to the farm house. The woman who lived there asked Bob, "Where do you want to go?"

Bob told her. Then she showed Bob which way to go.

When Bob finally got back to the lake, it was four o'clock, and his mom was waiting for him. Was she mad at him?

Bob won't be going on any field trips for a long time.

This is the end.

white   bone

1. On line I, write about what a brown fox was eating.

2. On line 2, write about what was eating an apple.

A small goat loved her jump rope. One day, she was jumping rope on the bank of a pond. A fox came by and took the rope from the goat. The goat said, "Oh please, Great Fox, give me my rope back."

The fox said, "No. I want to keep this rope."

The goat said, "Can I have the rope if I can pull it out of your paws?"

"Yes," the fox said, but the fox did not think that the goat could do that. So the goat pulled on the rope, and the fox pulled back really hard on the rope. Suddenly, the goat let go, and the fox fell into the pond. While he was getting out, the goat took the rope and ran to her house.

1. Who owned the jump rope?

2. Who took the rope away?

3. Did the goat pull the rope from the fox's hands?

4. Who tricked the fox by letting go of the rope?

5. What did the fox fall into?

113

1. sleekest
2. smashes
3. smokey
4. smoking
5. dumpy

1. <u>pushed</u>
2. <u>loved</u>
3. <u>friends</u>
4. <u>motors</u>
5. <u>puffed</u>

1. <u>ugly</u>
2. <u>perfect</u>
3. <u>mounted</u>
4. <u>nicer</u>
5. <u>slices</u>
6. <u>racing</u>

1. phew
2. bay
3. h<u>or</u>n
4. tug
5. honk
6. docks

1. rang
2. elm
3. sled
4. junk

Tubby the Tug
Part One

Bay Town got its name because it was on a big bay. Many, many ships and boats came in and out of the bay every day. There were boats with sails and boats with motors. Some of the fastest motorboats stayed at Dock Three. Those boats loved to show off. Each boat bragged that it was the fastest and the sleekest. But all of the boats knew that the boat named Red Cat was really the fastest and the sleekest.

All the other boats wanted to be friends with Red Cat. They liked to be seen near Red Cat. But when Red Cat was going as fast as he could go, no other boat in the bay could keep up with him. Red Cat would dart around the bar<u>ge</u>s and the slower ships.

Sometimes Red Cat would get very close to them, and the bar<u>ge</u>s and ships would blow their horns. But Red Cat didn't mind if the other boats got mad. What could they do about it?

One of the boats at Dock Three was as slow as Red Cat was fast. That boat was as dumpy as Red Cat was sleek. That boat was a smokey, old tug named Tubby. All the other boats said "Phew" when Tubby puffed in and out of the bay to do her work.

Most of the other boats were fun boats, but Tubby was a work boat. Tubby was ten times slower than Red Cat, but she was ten times stronger than Red Cat. Tubby's job was to pull and push the biggest ships in the bay.

Tubby was almost as strong as those large ships. And Tubby needed to be strong to keep the large ships from running into things. Tubby had to steer them away from places where the water was not deep. Also Tubby had to keep them from ramming into the docks. If a large ship runs into the docks, it keeps right on going and smashes everything in front of it until it finally stops.

This is not the end.

1. tear
2. wind
3. bow
4. does
5. lead
6. dove

fish   bird   green

1. On line 1, write about what is under the boat.

2. On line 2, write about what the red boat is under.

Peggy wanted to paint her room pink. So she got three pails of pink paint and some brushes. Peggy asked two of her pals to come and help her paint.

Each girl had a brush and a can of pink paint. Peggy started with the door, and her two pals painted the floor.

When they were done, Peggy was standing in the only part of the room that wasn't pink. "Help, help," Peggy said. "I'm stuck in my room."

Peggy's pals laughed, "You will have to stay there until the floor is dry."

But Peggy did not want to stay. She painted the part that wasn't pink. Then she walked across the wet paint. Now the room and Peggy's feet are pink.

1. What did Peggy want to paint?

2. Peggy wanted to paint it ▮▮▮▮ .

3. Peggy said, "I'm ▮▮▮▮ in my room."

4. How did Peggy get across the wet paint?

5. Now what things are pink?

20

114

1. barge
2. charge
3. boy
4. toy
5. sang
6. rang

1. <u>a</u>gain<u>s</u>t
2. <u>honk</u>ed
3. <u>block</u>s
4. <u>blow</u>n
5. a<u>wake</u>
6. bl<u>ast</u>

1. ugly
2. heavy
3. pushing
4. heading
5. puffing
6. bother

1. sport
2. sign
3. zone
4. add
5. trap
6. slept

Tubby the Tug
Part Two

It was six o'clock in the morning, and Tubby was starting her motor and puffing out smoke. The other boats at the dock woke up and started complaining. "We're trying to rest," they said. "What are you making all that racket for—and all that smoke? Phew."

"I can't help it," Tubby said. "I have to go to work."

"Well, go," Red Cat said. "And don't come back. I can't even nap when you're around. You smell bad."

So Tubby honked her horn three times and went off to push and pull the big ships in and out of the bay. The other boats got mad when Tubby honked her horn, but Tubby kept telling them, "I have to honk my horn three times when I start to work, and three times when I stop."

Around noon, the other boats at Dock Three came out to play. They darted around the bay and made waves. They laughed as they chased each other.

Tubby watched them, but only once in a while. The rest of the time, she had to watch what she was doing and where she was pushing ships and barges.

Once in a while, two or three of the fast boats would speed past Tubby and say something like, "Tubby, do you want to race?"

That would make Tubby feel bad. Tubby knew that a race with those boats would not be much of a contest. Tubby could not go very far in the time the other boats could go a mile.

So Tubby worked, and the other boats from Dock Three played. At the end of the day, when Tubby had put the last ship in place, she would honk her horn three times and go back to Dock Three. Tubby tried to keep her motor quiet so she wouldn't make too much smoke, but the other boats complained. "This is a no smoking dock," one of them yelled. "Get that smoking tug out of here."

One of the very sleek boats said to the boat next to it, "There goes one ugly boat. Phew."

Tubby went to the end of the dock and tried to rest. It wouldn't be long before Tubby had to go to work again.

More to come.

1. The old house had some lead pipes.
2. Dan went to live on a farm.
3. On the side of the road, two does ate grass.
4. We listened to live music at the park.
5. Jill took the lead near the end of the ra<u>ce</u>.
6. Before dinner, he does his chores.

1. On line 1, write about what a yellow bird is on.

2. On line 2, write about what is on green grass.

Dave and Bob were going to a party for their friend Jan. Bob and Dave were picking things to give Jan.

Dave said to Bob, "Jan will like what I give her more than she will like what you give her."

Bob said, "I do not care if Jan likes what you give her better. I just hope she likes all of the things she gets."

The day of the party, Jan and Dave and five of their friends were at the party. They were waiting for Bob to come before they cut the cake. Bob was late.

At last Bob came, and the cake was served. After everyone was done eating cake, Jan opened the things her friends bought her. Did she like what Dave bought her more? No. Dave and Bob gave her the same thing.

1. Who was the party for that Bob and Dave were going to?

2. Who wanted Jan to like all of the things her friends gave her?

3. What did they wait to do until Bob got there?

4. Why didn't Jan like what Dave gave her more than what Bob gave her?

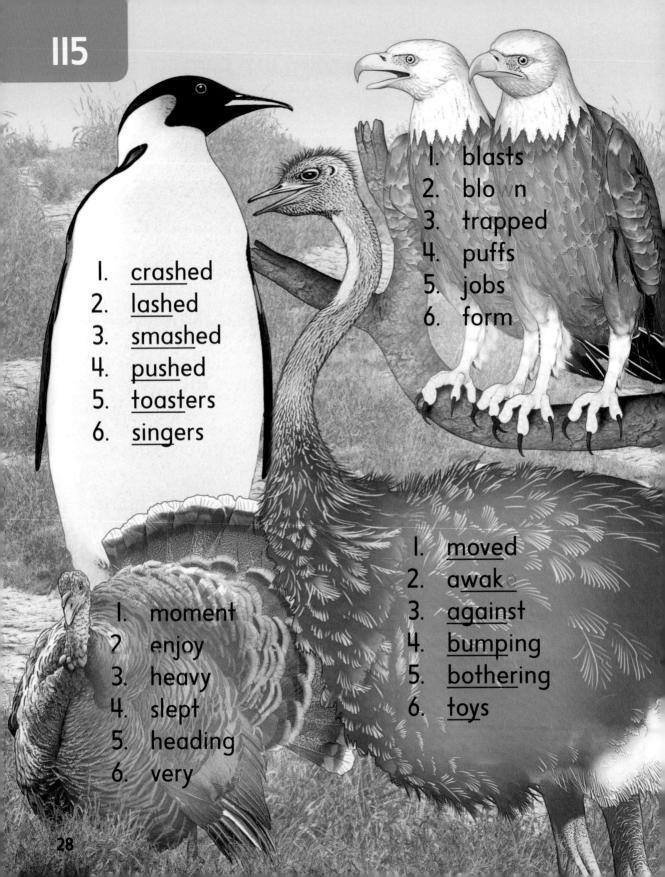

115

1. <u>crashed</u>
2. <u>lashed</u>
3. <u>smash</u>ed
4. <u>push</u>ed
5. <u>toa</u>sters
6. <u>sing</u>ers

1. blasts
2. blown
3. trapped
4. puffs
5. jobs
6. form

1. moment
2. enjoy
3. heavy
4. slept
5. heading
6. very

1. <u>moved</u>
2. a<u>wak</u>e
3. <u>agai</u>nst
4. <u>bump</u>ing
5. <u>bother</u>ing
6. <u>toy</u>s

Tubby the Tug
Part Three

That night, when Tubby and the other boats at Dock Three were sleeping, a very bad storm raced into the bay. The winds lashed out and rolled the water into large waves. Soon those waves were crashing against the docks. They were also crashing against the ships and barges. One barge that was longer than three blocks was blown out of place.

29

The wind and waves were pushing that barge right at Dock Three. Most of the speed boats were awake now, but the crashing waves had them trapped next to the dock. One of them saw the barge coming closer and closer to the dock. "Help, help," that boat called out. "Who can help me get free?"

The other boats were tugging at their ropes and shouting at each other. "Stop bumping into me," Red Cat shouted to the boat next to him.

"I can't help it," that boat said. "The waves are pushing me into you."

While all this was going on, Tubby was sleeping. All the wind and the waves were not bothering that big, old tug boat. She rocked a little, but she was ten times as heavy as the fun boats and didn't mind the wind and waves. So she slept.

The barge was very close to the dock now. It was so big that it made the dock look very small and made the boats look like little toys.

Then the barge made three loud horn blasts. Honk, honk, honk. It was trying to let everybody know that it was heading for the dock.

Those blasts woke Tubby. When Tubby heard them, she thought it was time to go to work. So Tubby quickly started her motor and let out three horn blasts. Red Cat and the others heard Tubby's blasts and saw the smoke. "Help us, Tubby. We're going to be smashed. Help us."

"Wow," Tubby said when she saw how close the barge was. "I don't know if I can stop that barge in time."

"Oh, please try. Please," the other boats cried.

More next time.

1. The singer took a bow after his song.
2. The dove was in a tree.
3. Jan made a bow with some string.
4. Beth likes to read before going to bed.
5. Tim dove from a branch in the tree.
6. Last week, the girls read about horses.

yellow   white

1. On line 1, write about what tires the green truck has.

2. On line 2, write about what has black tires.

Last summer, Ted had a job picking apples. Ted picked apples all day long. He picked red apples, and he picked green apples. Ted tried not to pick apples that had holes in them, apples that had brown spots, or apples with worms.

Every day after work, Ted got to take home all the apples he wanted. He ate some of the apples. With other apples, he made pies. He cooked the rest of the apples he took home and put them in jars and cans.

1. What was Ted's job last summer?
2. Ted picked red apples and ______ apples.
3. Were all of the apples good apples?
4. Ted took apples home. What did Ted do with the apples he didn't eat or make pies with?

116

1. b<u>oi</u>l
2. j<u>oi</u>n
3. p<u>oi</u>nt
4. v<u>oi</u>ce

1. <u>pushed</u>
2. <u>songs</u>
3. <u>doors</u>
4. <u>moved</u>
5. <u>moving</u>

1. act
2. smash
3. gray
4. m<u>ou</u>se
5. t<u>ea</u>se
6. c<u>ou</u>rse

1. lady
2. <u>valley</u>
3. <u>mountain</u>
4. <u>robot</u>
5. <u>apart</u>
6. <u>mixes</u>

1. nice
2. mice
3. p<u>ou</u>nce

Tubby the Tug
Part Four

A large barge was coming right at Dock Three. If something didn't stop that barge very soon, the barge would smash Red Cat and the other fun boats. "Help," Red Cat cried. "Please save us."

Tubby was trying to do that. The tug puffed out smoke and went as fast as she could.

"Honk, honk, honk." Tubby began pushing against the barge. But the barge kept moving closer and closer to Dock Three.

Tubby stayed between the barge and the dock and kept pushing against the side of the barge as hard as she could. But the barge kept going. It was coming closer and closer to the docks.

Tubby kept pushing and puffing and puffing and pushing. And the barge started moving slower and slower. Then it stopped. Then it moved slowly back. Tubby was pushing that barge against the waves and the wind. The other boats saw what Tubby was doing.

"Tubby saved us," Red Cat shouted.

The boats cheered and shouted, but Tubby still had a lot of work to do. After a long time, Tubby pushed that barge way out in the bay where it should be.

Tubby's motor worked so hard that parts of it started to burn up. When the barge was finally tied up in place again, Tubby stopped out there in the bay. "Honk, honk, honk." The other boats knew that Tubby's motor had blown up.

"I'll save Tubby," Red Cat said as he finally got free from the dock. Red Cat raced out into the bay, grabbed Tubby's tow rope, and pulled the little tug back to the dock. Red Cat never worked so hard before, but he was glad to do it.

Today, Tubby's motor is fixed so only a little smoke comes out when she works really hard. And Tubby has a coat of bright red paint, just like Red Cat. And Tubby has a place right next to Red Cat at Dock Three. Tubby still honks, puffs a little smoke, and goes to work every morning. But the other boats don't complain. And no boats make fun of Tubby as they speed by. They wave and say the things that pals say when they see each other. "How are you doing?" They are proud to have Tubby as their friend.

The end.

girl   gray

1. On line 1, write about what hat a man wore.

2. On line 2, write about who wore a green hat.

There was a barge that didn't like tug boats. The barge said, "Those tugs are always bumping into my side and trying to push me around."

One day, the barge was going into a bay when a tug boat came near. The barge said, "I don't need your help. I can find a good place in the bay myself."

Just then a big wind pushed the barge all the way to shore. "Help, help," the barge called. "Who can pull me away from the shore?"

The tug said, "I could do it. But you'll have to be nice to me." The barge agreed. So the tug pulled the barge away from the shore. Now the tug and the barge are good friends.

1. Who did not like tugs?

2. A wind came up when the barge was heading into a ▨▨▨.

3. That wind pushed the barge all the way to the ▨▨▨.

4. Who pulled the barge away from the shore?

5. Now the tug and the barge are ▨▨▨.

117

L
1. <u>sounded</u>
2. <u>following</u>
3. <u>mountains</u>
4. <u>valleys</u>
5. <u>any</u>where
6. <u>paint</u>ing

A
1. phone
2. of course
3. rule
4. sorry
5. lovely
6. robot

M
1. p<u>oi</u>nt
2. v<u>oi</u>ce
3. b<u>oi</u>l

S
1. spent
2. moment
3. ray
4. gray
5. nice
6. mice

P
1. slic<u>es</u>
2. pe<u>o</u>ple
3. perfect
4. toaster
5. family
6. matter

Rolla Slows Down

When we left Rolla, she was very happy. She was number 1. She went up and down at the right speed. The music sounded fine. The children were happy, and their mothers were happy.

Things went on like this for weeks. But then one day, something happened. Rolla said to herself, "I am number 1, but I am right behind number 8." Rolla thought that she should be far away from number 8. Then it would look as if she was the leader and the other horses were following her.

Rolla said, "I will get far from horse 8." To do that, Rolla slowed down. She went slower, and slower, and slower. But of course her plan didn't work. When she went slower, all of the other horses went slower. The music slowed down and sounded awful. The mothers were unhappy. One of them said, "This merry-go-round is so slow, you can't tell if it's going or if it has stopped."

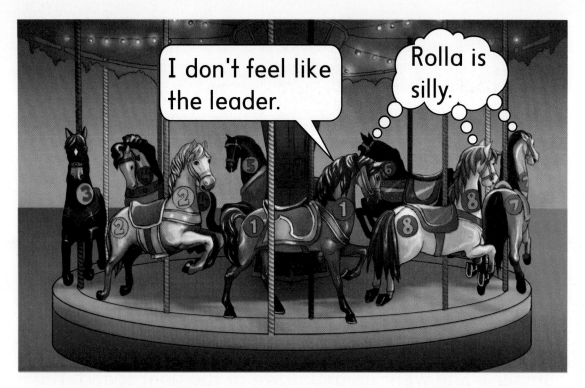

The other horses were not happy with Rolla. Horse 2 kept shouting at Rolla, "Come on, Rolla. Let's get this merry-go-round moving." But Rolla tried as hard as she could to keep going slowly.

At the end of the day, horse 8 was still there, right in front of Rolla.

That evening, horse number 3 asked, "What are you trying to do?"

When Rolla told them, some of the horses started to laugh. Then horse number 5 said, "Rolla would you be happy if you could not see horse 8?"

"Yes," Rolla said. "If I could not see that horse, I would not feel like I was following it. I would feel like the leader."

So the other horses got together and did a lot of talking. When they were done, they smiled and told Rolla they would fix things so she would feel like the leader.

The next day when Rolla woke up, she looked in front of her and saw mountains and valleys. They were lovely. She couldn't see another horse anywhere in front of her. After a while, she <u>fou</u>nd out that the other horses had made a painting and put it between her and horse 8. But Rolla didn't care. She felt wonderful leading the other horses into the mountains.

So everything is fine now. The horses are happy. The music sounds good. And the mothers and children like the merry-go-round even more than before.

The end.

1. Before the storm, the wind was howling.

2. There were live baboons at the zoo.

3. Bob had a big tear on his cheek.

4. You have to wind old clocks and watches.

5. The book had a large tear in it.

6. Some baboons live at the zoo.

---

small

1. On line 1, write about what kind of fins the red fish has.

2. On line 2, write about what kind of fins the green fish has.

Two ants named Tam and Sid lived far away from each other. They were best friends. But it took a lot of work to see each other, because they lived so far apart. One day, Tam would have to walk all the way to Sid's house and back. The next day, Sid would have to walk all the way to Tam's house and back. Those are very long walks for ants.

One day, Sid came up with a plan. Sid said, "We could both start walking to each other's house and meet somewhere in between. That way, we wouldn't have to walk as far."

So the ants tried that. But it didn't work. Sid didn't see Tam, and Tam didn't see Sid. Sid ended up at Tam's house, and Tam ended up at Sid's house.

1. Did Tam and Sid live far away from each other?

2. Who thought of a plan to meet somewhere in between Sid's and Tam's houses?

3. Did the plan work?

4. Where did Tam end up?

5. Where did Sid end up?

118

1. mice
2. slice
3. voice
4. choice
5. toys
6. boys

1. folding
2. corner
3. recall
4. dishes
5. toaster
6. moment

1. Molly
2. Bleep
3. perfect
4. robot
5. hello
6. hung

1. tiny
2. nasty
3. tigers
4. phone
5. people

1. elm
2. sort
3. boomed
4. seats
5. hawks

Molly and Bleep
Part One

Molly was a very smart woman. She made a lot of things that were very smart. She made toasters and folding chairs and even racing boats. But none of the things she made were perfect. Her toaster toasted six slices at the same time, but three of them were too dark. Her folding chairs sometimes folded when someone was sitting in them. A friend of Molly's sat in one of her folding chairs. She was stuck in it for a long time before Molly found her.

Molly's racing boats were very fast and very strong. When they were going very fast, they were wonderful. But when they slowed down, they would get so low in the water that a little wave could sink them.

The best thing that Molly made was a robot
named Bleep. She worked on Bleep every day in her
shop. It took her six years to make that robot. When
she was done, Bleep was almost perfect.

Bleep could get the mail, go to the store, and ride
a bike. He could also do many things you told him to
do. He could even speak. His voice sounded just like
Molly's. But when Bleep spoke, he did some things
that Molly did not do. Most of the time, Bleep started
talking by saying, "Bleep." And when someone told
Bleep to do something, he would say, "Okay, baby."

Bleep could also talk on the phone and tell Molly what people said. If the phone rang while Molly was working on her folding chair or her racing boat, Bleep would talk on the phone. Later he would tell Molly what the person said. But Bleep would sometimes tell big lies. One time, Bleep talked on the phone and then said to Molly, "Bleep. Your mother just called. She found four tigers in her front yard."

More to come.

1. Sweetie saw a dove at the bird bath.
2. Debby likes to read books about far away places.
3. In Bonnie's yard, Sweetie dove at birds.
4. Before eating dinner, Sam does his homework.
5. Al worked on math before he read the story.
6. Jill saw five does in her back yard.

1. On line 1, write about what kind of vehicle the small man drives.

2. On line 2, write about what kind of man drives a brown truck.

A boy named Rob was always thinking. He would think in the morning. He would think when he ate lunch. He would think at school and at home. One day, his sister said to Rob, "Why do you spend so much time thinking?"

Rob said, "I don't know. Let me think about that."

So Rob thought about why he thought. This went on for five days.

Then he told his sister, "I don't know why I think so much. But I think I'm tired of thinking. Let's do something else."

So they went bike riding.

1. Who always thought?

2. He thought at home and in ███████ .

3. Who asked him why he thought so much?

4. Did Rob know why he thought so much?

5. What did Rob and his sister do after Rob got tired of thinking?

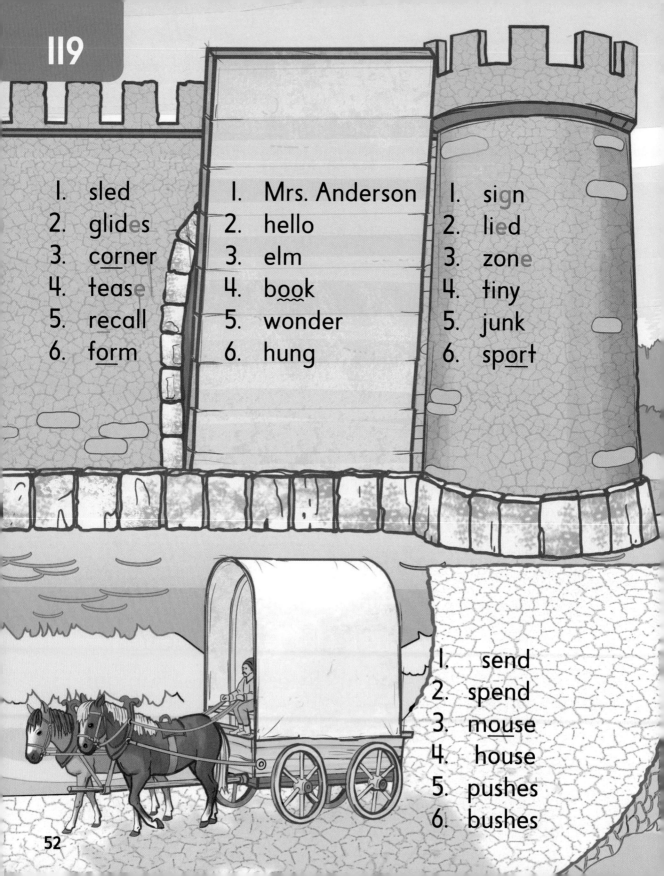

1. sled
2. glides
3. corner
4. tease
5. recall
6. form

1. Mrs. Anderson
2. hello
3. elm
4. book
5. wonder
6. hung

1. sign
2. lied
3. zone
4. tiny
5. junk
6. sport

1. send
2. spend
3. mouse
4. house
5. pushes
6. bushes

Molly and Bleep
Part Two

Bleep was a robot that was almost perfect. But he did one thing that was not perfect. Sometimes he told big lies. And sometimes those lies made a big mess.

The biggest mess that Bleep made happened when Mrs. Anderson called. She was a friend of Molly's. She had never met Bleep or heard his voice. Molly was in her shop working on a racing sled. Bleep was washing the dishes. When the phone rang, Bleep picked it up and said, "Bleep. Hello."

Mrs. Anderson did not know that she was talking to Bleep. She thought she was talking to Molly. So she said, "You know that we are to meet for lunch today."

Bleep said, "Bleep. Yes."

Mrs. Anderson said, "Well, it is your turn to pick a place where we will eat. Where do you want to go?"

Bleep said, "Bleep. I like the place on the corner of First and Elm."

Mrs. Anderson said, "First and Elm? I don't recall anything on that corner."

Bleep said, "Bleep. It is a fine place. You will like it a lot."

Mrs. Anderson said, "Well then, I will see you on the corner of First and Elm around noon." Then she said, "Could you also bring that book you wanted me to read?"

Bleep said, "Okay, baby."

Bleep hung up the phone and went back to washing the dishes. Pretty soon, Molly came in from her shop. She asked, "Did anyone call for me?"

Bleep said, "Bleep. Yes. Mrs. Anderson called about lunch today."

"Good," Molly said, "Where does she want to eat?"

Bleep said, "Bleep. The corner of First and Elm."

Molly said, "First and Elm? I don't recall a place to eat on that corner."

Bleep said, "Bleep. Mrs. Anderson said that it is a wonderful place to eat. Yum, yum."

Molly said, "That sounds good. Did she say anything else?"

Bleep said, "Bleep. Mrs. Anderson says that you should bring one of your folding chairs."

Molly shook her head. "I wonder why she wants a chair."

More to come.

1. Joan took a bow after she spoke to the crowd.

2. A tree fell over in a big wind.

3. They don't make toys with lead in them anymore.

4. The boat workers wind ropes around poles.

5. The black horse took the lead on the last lap.

6. Don tied the string into a bow.

---

car

1. On line I, write about what the brown cat sat on.

2. On line 2, write about what sat on a leaf.

Sandy was not very good at math. When she wanted to make a six, she would make a nine. When she wanted to write a two, she would make a five. Sandy also had a hard time with math problems. If the problem said to add six and two, Sandy could not put down the right numbers. She would add nine and five.

Sandy was sad. She asked her teacher to help her with her math. So her teacher worked with Sandy. Now Sandy is very good at math. She no longer mixes up six and nine, or two and five. Before long, Sandy could work any math problem that her teacher gave. She could even add three numbers at a time.

1. What was Sandy poor at?

2. Which number did Sandy write for six?

3. Which number did Sandy write for two?

4. Who helped Sandy get better at math?

$1 + 7 =$ $4 + 2 =$

$3 + 1 =$ $5 + 5 =$

1. maker
2. lady
3. sign
4. zone
5. teased
6. tonight

1. rule
2. sorry
3. junk
4. sport
5. rods
6. act

1. family
2. giggle
3. matter
4. parked
5. pounce
6. choice

1. lemur
2. mouse
3. bone
4. fins
5. bats
6. skin

58

Molly and Bleep
Part Three

Bleep talked on the phone and told Mrs. Anderson one big lie. Then Bleep talked to Molly and told her two big lies.

Molly did not know why Mrs. Anderson wanted a folding chair, but Molly told Bleep to load the chair into her van. Molly loved her van. It was red, and it was big. So it had lots of room for the things that Molly needed when she made something like a racing sled or a cake maker.

Molly drove her red van to the corner of First and Elm. She didn't see a place to eat. She didn't see Mrs. Anderson's car. The only thing she saw was a big junk yard. So she parked her vehicle by the fence in front of the junk yard. There was a sign on the fence. That sign said "Drop Off Zone." Molly didn't know what a drop off zone was.

Molly got out of her vehicle and walked along Elm Street. She was looking for Mrs. Anderson or the place where they would eat. But all she saw was a great junk yard. Molly kept walking and looking for Mrs. Anderson's car. That car was very easy to see. It was bright red, just like Molly's van. But Mrs. Anderson's car was a small sport car, not a big van.

While Molly was looking for Mrs. Anderson, Mrs. Anderson drove up to the corner of First and Elm. She saw Molly's van in the drop off zone. So she parked next to the van. Then she got out and started to look for Molly. She said to herself, "It is hard to believe that there is a good place to eat on this street." But she walked down Elm Street. At last she saw Molly.

Mrs. Anderson called to Molly and said, "Where is there a place to eat around here?"

Molly said, "I don't know. Bleep said you wanted to come here."

"Not so," Mrs. Anderson said. "When we talked on the phone, you told me that you wanted to come here."

Molly said, "Oh dear. You didn't talk to me on the phone. You talked to Bleep. I think Bleep lied to both of us."

This is not the end.

1. On line I, write about what a girl did in the yellow car.

2. On line 2, write about what slept in the red van.

Jane and her pals got into Jane's van and went down town. They went to hear some singers who were really good. Lots of people were there to listen to the singers. When Jane and her pals sat down, it was just about time for the singing to start.

The singers came out and sang two songs. As they were singing the third song, suddenly, one of them sneezed. Then the rest of them sneezed. The singers sneezed until the end of the song. Jane and her pals liked the sneezing song a lot. As Jane and her pals cheered, they started to sneeze too. Before long, everybody was sneezing.

1. Who did Jane go with?

2. Who did they hear?

3. How many songs did they sing without sneezing?

4. Did Jane and her pals like the sneezing song?

5. What did everyone do after that song?

122

1. letting
2. apart
3. belonged
4. enjoy
5. lemurs
6. together

1. carry
2. nasty
3. sorry
4. lady
5. family
6. stinky

1. tickle
2. pickle
3. friend
4. spend
5. phones
6. bones

1. edge
2. hall
3. rule
4. sort
5. shadow
6. here's

Molly and Bleep
Part Four

Molly and Mrs. Anderson found out that Bleep had lied to both of them.

They laughed about it. Molly said, "I'll have to be careful about letting Bleep talk on the phone."

Then Molly and Mrs. Anderson started to walk back to the corner of First and Elm.

When they got back to the drop off zone, Molly said, "Where is my van?"

Mrs. Anderson said, "Where is my car?"

Molly and Mrs. Anderson saw a worker, so they called to him and asked about the cars.

The junk yard worker said, "Here's the rule about the drop off zone. If vehicles are left in the drop off zone, we take them apart. Your cars were in the drop off zone. So your vehicles are no longer vehicles."

"No longer vehicles?" Mrs. Anderson shouted. "You can't take my car apart."

The worker said, "Sorry. We just followed the rule about vehicles in the drop off zone."

Then the worker led Molly and Mrs. Anderson inside the junk yard. He took them to a large pile of vehicle parts. He said, "Well, this pile is what is left of your car and van."

That door goes to the van.

Mrs. Anderson said, "This is awful." She turned to the worker and said, "You took the cars apart, so now you can put them back together, just the way they were."

"Sorry, lady," the worker said, "We just take things apart. We don't know how to put them back together."

Mrs. Anderson started to cry.

Molly said, "I am pretty good at making things. If we can get some of the workers to help us, we can get these vehicles back together before it is time for dinner."

Four workers helped. Mrs. Anderson helped too. Molly was in charge. She told the others where to put the rods and the doors and the other vehicle parts.

More to come.

1. On line 1, write about who drank from a little cup.

2. On line 2, write about what a girl drank from.

Many things look like they are flying when they are gliding. When something glides, it rides on air. Something that's flying pushes air to move itself.

Hawks fly and glide.

Here's a picture of a hawk flying. It is flapping its wings to push air and move itself.

Here's a picture of a hawk gliding. The hawk is not flapping its wings. It's just riding on the air.

An airplane has a motor to push the air so it will move. So airplanes that use their motor in the air are flying.

A plane that is in the air, but doesn't have the motor running, is gliding. At least the folks inside the plane better hope it is gliding.

1. Something that is riding on air is ▆▆▆▆ .
2. Something that is pushing air to move is ▆▆▆▆ .
3. What animal can fly and glide?
 • moose   • snakes   • hawks   • seals
4. What part of an airplane makes it fly?

123

1. s<u>or</u>t
2. cheeks
3. brav<u>e</u>
4. job
5. fli<u>ck</u>
6. h<u>all</u>

1. afraid
2. lemur
3. putting
4. tickle
5. giggle
6. ugly

1. enj<u>oy</u>
2. ex<u>plain</u>
3. bel<u>onged</u>
4. to<u>night</u>
5. <u>together</u>
6. <u>party</u>

1. warn
2. kitchen
3. ceiling
4. knock
5. knew
6. new

Molly and Bleep
Part Five

Molly, Mrs. Anderson, and four workers from the junk yard put the van and car back together. By dinner time, there were two red vehicles inside the junk yard, but those two vehicles were not the same as the vehicles that drove up to the junk yard. There was no longer a van and a little sport car. There were two vehicles that were part van and part sport car.

One of the vehicles looked like a van in front and a sport car in back. The other vehicle looked like a sport car in front and a van in back. That one had two seats and Molly's folding chair in it. Mrs. Anderson looked again at the vehicles and started to cry once more.

Molly said, "Well, I did the best I could, but all the parts were red. So I didn't always know which part belonged to which vehicle." The workers were laughing pretty hard. One of them said, "Those are two ugly cars."

Mrs. Anderson cried, "Yes, very ugly."

Molly said, "I don't know. I think those vehicles look sort of pretty."

The workers laughed harder than before.

Molly told Mrs. Anderson, "Well, pick one of these things, and I'll take the other."

So Mrs. Anderson drove home in one of the red things. At home she cried and cried. Molly drove home in the other red thing. Then she looked at it a long time and said to herself, "Those workers are right. This thing is ugly."

When Molly went inside, Bleep said, "Bleep. Did you enjoy lunch?"

Molly said, "No, I didn't." For a moment, she thought about taking Bleep back to the junk yard and leaving him in the drop off zone. But then she said, "From now on, you may not talk on the phone."

Bleep said, "Okay, baby."

The next day, three workers, Molly, and Bleep put the vehicles back together the right way. The workers were from a car shop. One of them was very good at putting cars together. He told Molly and the others how to put the parts together and where they went. When the job was done, Mrs. Anderson was very happy, and so was Molly.

The end.

cow	glass

1. On line 1, write about what the cat drank water from.

2. On line 2, write about what drank water from a pail.

A snail wanted to swim. She went into a stream. Did she swim? No. She just sank to the bottom. She didn't have any arms or legs to swim with, so she had to creep along the bottom of the stream until she could get out of the water. That was no fun.

The next day, she tried to swim again. She went to another part of the stream and went in. Did she swim? No. She sank to the bottom of the stream, again. The snail just could not swim.

On the third day, the snail asked a turtle, "Could I sit on your back while you go swimming?"

The turtle said, "Yes." So the snail got on the turtle's back, and they went swimming. The snail said, "I knew I could enjoy swimming. That was fun."

1. What did a snail want to do?
2. Was the snail able to swim on her own?
3. On the first day, the snail got out of the stream by creeping along the ▆▆▆▆ .
4. Did the snail try to swim the next day?
5. Who helped the snail?

124

1. <u>e</u>w
2. n<u>e</u>w
3. f<u>e</u>w
4. ch<u>e</u>w
5. fl<u>e</u>w

1. <u>a</u>fraid
2. <u>t</u>onight
3. <u>bed</u>room
4. <u>tick</u>le
5. <u>n</u>asty
6. <u>paint</u>ings

1. Patty
2. Arnold
3. paw
4. matt<u>er</u>
5. gig<u>gl</u>e
6. boom<u>ed</u>

1. fa<u>c</u>e
2. l<u>ou</u>dly
3. sn<u>ea</u>king
4. gr<u>ay</u>
5. poun<u>ce</u>
6. <u>ch</u>eeks

Patty and the Cats
Part One

There was once a very large mouse named Patty. She lived with her mom and dad and her six brothers and nine sisters.

All the other mice in her family were nice and quiet. Each one spoke in a tiny voice. When the house was dark at night, they snuck around without making a sound.

Patty did not act like the others in her family. She could not speak in a tiny voice. Even when she tried to speak in a whisper, her voice was loud.

When she went with the others at night, she spoke so loudly that she scared them. They were scared because a large gray cat named Arnold lived in the house. If Arnold found the mice while they were sneaking around looking for food, he would pounce on them. When Patty said something at night, her brothers and sisters would say, "Shshshsh." But no matter how hard she tried to talk quietly, her voice boomed out.

Patty's brothers gave her the name, "Big Mouse the Big Mouth." She didn't like that name, but her voice was too loud. And if her brothers teased her too much, she could just say, "Please stop teasing me," and her voice would blow them over.

More next time.

1. On line 1, write about what a black bug is on.
2. On line 2, write about what is on a yellow flower.

Seth was a fox who lived with his mother and dad. His mother and dad asked Seth to leave because he did not clean up after himself. Seth left his house and walked around the forest looking for another place to live.

Seth found a mole who lived under the ground near a tree. Seth told the mole why he had to leave home. The mole told Seth, "I am good at cleaning up, but I don't know how to cook."

Seth said, "I am a good cook." So Seth moved in with the mole. Seth cooked for the mole and the mole worked with Seth to clean up. Seth and the mole were both happy.

1. What kind of animal was Seth?

2. Seth's mom and dad asked him to leave because he didn't ▓▓▓▓ after himself.

3. Who cooked?

4. Who cleaned?

5. Are Seth and the mole happy now?

125

1. chew
2. blew
3. news

1. cheeks
2. smells
3. halls
4. thoughts

1. <u>visiting</u>
2. <u>party</u>
3. <u>shadows</u>
4. <u>living</u>
5. <u>juggle</u>
6. <u>settle</u>

1. tent
2. melt
3. noise
4. expert
5. louder
6. shouting

1. toward
2. warn
3. through
4. circus
5. cycle
6. kitchen

Patty and the Cats
Part Two

Patty could not speak in a soft voice. But if you think her talking voice was loud, you should have heard her shouting voice. It was many times louder. That shouting voice was so loud that it shook the house. It made anybody near Patty have ringing ears.

One time, she was playing with some of her brothers and sisters. They started to tickle her, and she started to giggle. Then she started to laugh and shout. She shouted so loudly that she sent two of her sisters sailing into the air. Three of her brothers had such ringing ears that they did not hear well for six days.

That night, Patty was getting ready to go out with her family when her mom gave her some very bad news. "Patty," her mom said. "You can't go out with us tonight. It is just not safe."

"Oh, please let me go," Patty said. "I'll be quiet. I won't say a word."

"I'm sorry," her mom said. "You have to stay inside our home."

Patty was very sad, but she did what her mom said. She watched the others go out. She felt big tears form in her eyes and run down her cheeks.

Patty's mom and dad were afraid because there were new smells in the house. Those were the smells of new cats. The mice didn't know it, but Arnold had four friends that were visiting him. They were large, nasty cats who loved to chase mice and pounce on them.

This is not the end.

Mammals live on land or in water. Some land mammals spend most of their time in trees. Some of these mammals can glide from tree to tree.

Here is a picture of a flying lemur.

Flying lemurs don't really fly, they just glide. Here are pictures of two other gliding mammals.

There is only one mammal that can fly without a machine. The only mammal that can do more than glide and really fly is a bat. Bats don't have feathers. Their wings are made of skin.

1. Does a flying lemur really fly?
2. When flying lemurs are in the air, what are they really doing?
3. Is there one or more than one kind of mammal that can glide?
4. How many kinds of mammals can fly?
5. What are those mammals called?

cat   yellow

1. On line I, write about what kind of tape is on a pink sail.
2. On line 2, write about what has red tape on it.

126

1. expl<u>ai</u>n
2. p<u>aw</u>
3. p<u>ar</u>ty
4. e<u>dge</u>

1. <u>ce</u>iling
2. knocked
3. climb
4. warn
5. kitchen
6. joy

1. flick
2. cheese
3. brave
4. shadow
5. melt
6. west

1. toward
2. through
3. shoe

1. <u>freezer</u>
2. <u>pouncing</u>
3. <u>noises</u>
4. <u>letter</u>
5. <u>cycles</u>
6. <u>arguing</u>

Patty and the Cats
Part Three

Arnold had asked four friends to come over to his place. He told them that his house had lots of mice and that the cats would have a great pouncing party.

Patty was inside her home, looking out the mouse hole at her family. She could see her dad lead the way toward the kitchen. The others followed slowly along the edge of the rug in the living room. Then they snuck down the hall.

Suddenly, Patty saw something that gave her a great scare. It was the shadow of a cat, then another shadow and another. Three cats were following Patty's family into the kitchen.

Patty said to herself, "I must do something to save my family." Patty thought for a moment and then snuck through the mouse hole. She went along the edge of the rug and down the hall. She was now behind the three cats, and the three cats were behind Patty's family.

Patty was going to tell her family, "Cats are behind you. Run." But just as she was going to warn the others, she saw shadows on the other side of the kitchen. There were two more cats in front of Patty's family waiting for them. If the mice started to run, they would run right into the cats who were waiting.

All five cats were slowly moving toward her family. One of the cats behind the mice was getting very close to one of Patty's sisters. That cat was getting ready to pounce.

More to come.

hill   tree

1. On line 1, write about what the bird has a home in.

2. On line 2, write about what the ant has a home in.

The bragging rats were arguing about who could jump higher. The bragging rat with big yellow teeth said, "I can jump over tree tops." The other bragging rat said, "I will cook you food for a week if you jump over a tree top."

The rat with the yellow teeth walked up to a baby tree that was only one foot tall. The rat with yellow teeth smiled at the other bragging rat and went to jump over the baby tree top. That bragging rat jumped only three inches in the air. He hit the baby tree top and fell back into the dirt.

Did the rat with the long tail have to cook for a week? No! But most of the rats had a good laugh.

1. What did the bragging rat with big yellow teeth say he could jump over?

2. If he did that, how long did the other bragging rat say he'd cook for?

3. How tall was the tree the rat with yellow teeth tried to jump over?

4. How high did the rat with yellow teeth jump?

5. Most of the rats had a good ███████.

127

1. mir<u>ro</u>r
2. b<u>ou</u>nce
3. crawled
4. c<u>u</u>rled
5. n<u>oi</u>se
6. win

1. <u>trapez</u>e
2. <u>ex</u>plained
3. <u>loudest</u>
4. <u>carry</u>
5. <u>deeper</u>

1. paws
2. claws
3. blew
4. flew

5. towns
6. clowns

1. circus
2. through
3. ceiling
4. knocked
5. watching

1. cheese
2. brave
3. flick
4. kit<u>e</u>s
5. expert
6. chan<u>g</u>ed

Patty and the Cats
Part Four

Patty's family was in the kitchen of the house. Behind them were three cats. In front of them were two more cats. One of the cats was getting ready to pounce on Patty's sister.

Patty tried to think, but her thoughts were mixed up. She just stood there in the dark, watching the cat flick his tail. Now the cat was starting to leap. Patty could see the sharp claws that were out on the pouncing cat's front paws.

Without thinking, Patty shouted in her loudest
voice, "WATCH OUT."

The room shook so hard that two paintings
fell off the wall. The pouncing cat had planned to
jump one foot high and land on Patty's sister. That
cat jumped 8 feet high and hit his head against the
ceiling. Then he landed on the kitchen table.

Patty's voice sent the other four cats flying too. When those cats landed, they were howling and running away as fast as they could go.

The mice had been knocked into a pile against the kitchen wall. Slowly they picked themselves up and followed Patty back to their mouse home.

When the mice were safe inside their home, Patty explained why she had shouted. Everybody in her family looked at her without saying a word. They didn't talk because they couldn't hear anything that Patty said.

Three days later, when the mice could hear again, they gave Patty a cheese party. Her dad said, "We are very pr_ou_d of you. You are a brav_e_ mouse, and you saved us from those cats. Thank you."

Patty had tears in her eyes again. But they were tears of joy. From that day on, Patty went everywhere with her family. They didn't mind Patty being loud because they knew a blast from her big voice would keep them safe.

The end.

boy

1. On line 1, write about who draws with a green pen.
2. On line 2, write about what a girl writes with.

A man woke up one night. He thought he heard a no͟i͟se. He snuck from his bedroom into the dark hall. When he got to the end of the hall, he looked around the corner. He saw a fac͜e looking back at him. The man yelled and turned on the lights.

When the man looked around the corner again, he didn't see anyone. What he saw was a painting of himself hanging on the wall.

The man felt silly. He said to himself, "I forgot that painting was there. I will remember that painting next time."

Then he went back to sleep.

1. The man got up because he thought he heard ▬▬▬.

2. The first time the man looked around the corner, what did he see?

3. How did that make the man feel?

4. The man really saw a painting of ▬▬▬.

5. Will the man try to remember that painting next time?

128

1. liar
2. violin
3. unicycle
4. argue
5. argument
6. porch

1. ad
2. noise
3. tent
4. tight
5. bounced
6. threw

1. circus
2. trapeze
3. juggle
4. settle
5. newspaper
6. perform

1. Sherlock
2. Moe
3. nothing
4. expert

TICKETS

1. bull
2. few
3. rubbed
4. scrub
5. sniff
6. south

The Circus
Part One

The names of the bragging rats were Sherlock and Moe. The rat with big yellow teeth was known as Moe. The rat with the long tail was known as Sherlock. Moe and Sherlock had not bragged for a year. Their last fight was about which rat could bake the best pie.

A new fight started one spring day, over a year after the baking contest. Sherlock and Moe were looking at an ad that was on the ground. The ad was for a circus.

Moe said, "I can do circus tricks better than anybody else in the world. I can walk the tight rope. I can juggle anything. And I am an expert at riding a unicycle."

Sherlock said, "You think you're an expert. I am the expert. I can do tricks on the trapeze that you have never even seen before. I can juggle 12 nuts at once. I can . . ."

"That's nothing," Moe shouted. "I can juggle 40 nuts while I am on a trapeze doing tricks that nobody has ever seen before."

The rats shouted for a long time. The other rats in the pack were getting very tired of the noise and the lies.

At last, the wise old rat walked over to the bragging rats and said, "Be quiet. There is a way to settle this. We will have a circus. And then we will see which of you does the best circus tricks."

So all the rats in the pack worked together very hard to set up a circus tent with a tight rope, a trapeze, unicycles, and lots of things to juggle. The next day, it would be time for the bragging rats to show off their circus tricks.

More next time.

brown

1. On line 1, write about which dog lived in a pink house.
2. On line 2, write about which house a small dog lived in.

107

Winter was almost over, and Jan was sad. She loved to sled in the snow. She loved to hike in the snow. She just loved snow. But she knew that soon the snow would melt. She said to herself, "I will save some snow so I can have it later." She gathered up large piles of snow and took them to a place where the snow would not melt.

Later that day, Jan's mother came home from the store. She had food to put in the freezer. But when she opened up the freezer, she saw that there was no room for the food. The freezer was filled up with snow. Jan's mom was not very happy. And Jan had to take all that snow out of the freezer.

1. Jan was sad because winter was almost ▨▨▨.

2. What did Jan love?

3. Where did Jan put snow?

4. What did Jan's mom have to put in the freezer?

1. carry
2. closed
3. bounced
4. cloth
5. nip
6. swung

1. perform
2. expert
3. laughter
4. eaten
5. juggling
6. argue

1. waddled
2. sniffing
3. planting
4. falling
5. meanest
6. middle

1. eight
2. through
3. threw
4. answer
5. shoes
6. honey

1. bull
2. dot
3. clown
4. climbed
5. ladder
6. asleep

Today we will have a contest.

The Circus
Part Two

It was the day of the circus. Moe and Sherlock were still arguing. Moe said, "It's going to be so easy to beat you that I could do it with one eye closed and with one leg tied up."

"Oh yeah?" Sherlock said. "I could beat you while I was asleep with two legs tied up."

All the rats from the pack and rats from other packs gathered in the circus tent. The wise old rat said, "Today we will have a contest of circus tricks. Behind me are the two rats who will perform. You will watch them perform. Then you'll vote for which of the rats is the best at doing circus tricks."

The first contest was juggling. Moe started out with four nuts. He threw all four in the air. Two landed on his head. Two landed on the floor. None landed in his paws.

The crowd roared with laughter.

Sherlock started out with four nuts. He threw them into the air. Three nuts hit him on the head. One nut landed on the floor, <u>bounced</u> up, and landed in his paw. He said, "That is what I planned to do."

The crowd laughed.

The wise old rat said, "For the next contest, the rats will ride unicycles."

Both bragging rats tried to ride at the same time. They got on. They ran into each other. They fell down. Then they did a lot of yelling at each other. "You knocked me down. Stay out of my way."

The crowd laughed a lot.

This story is not over.

black

1. On line 1, write about what a yellow chair was on.
2. On line 2, write about what was on a green rug.

One day, Henry said to himself, "I think I will go for a long walk." So he started to walk. He walked from his house to the other side of town. When he got there, he said, "I think I'll just keep on walking." And that's what he did. He walked all day long. At the end of the day, he said, "I don't want to walk any more." So he stopped right where he was.

He was next to a farm house. After a while, the farmer came out and said, "Why don't you go back home?"

Henry said, "Because I don't want to walk any more."

The farmer said, "Well, then, why don't you run home?"

Henry liked that plan. So he ran home.

1. One day, Henry went for a long ▨▨▨▨ .
2. Did he stop walking when he got to the other side of town?
3. When he finally stopped, he was near a ▨▨▨▨ .
4. Did he want to walk any more?
5. So how did he get home?

1. east
2. west
3. porch
4. change
5. flew
6. swoops

1. ladder
2. ouch
3. night
4. snooze
5. yawn
6. few

1. tightly
2. climbing
3. crawling
4. polite
5. noisy
6. oldest

1. gone
2. hour
3. sure
4. school
5. violin
6. shoes

1. alarm
2. spite
3. amaze
4. clown
5. vote
6. kennel

The Circus
Part Three

After the bragging rats tried to juggle and ride unicycles, they tried walking the tight rope.

Moe climbed the ladder and was getting ready to go on the tight rope. He looked scared. Then he said. "Oh, I forgot my tight rope shoes. So I can't do it." The crowd laughed.

As Moe started to climb back down the ladder, he slipped and fell. The crowd laughed even more.

Sherlock said, "You don't even know how to walk on a tight rope. Watch me."

Sherlock climbed the ladder and crawled out on the tight rope. Then he slipped and was hanging by one paw. Then he was yelling and hanging by no paws. Ouch. He landed on the floor, and the crowd laughed. Sherlock stood up and said, "That's what I wanted to do." The crowd laughed harder.

The last contest was the trapeze. Both rats climbed
up the same ladder and tried to get on the same trapeze.
Soon both of them were hanging by one paw. Then they
were hanging by no paws. Boom. Ouch.

The rats in the crowd laughed so loudly that
they could not hear the bragging rats yelling at each
other. "You got in my way. I was getting ready to do a
great trick."

"No, you got in my way."

After the laughter stopped, everybody voted for the
rat that did the best circus tricks.

Did one of the bragging rats win the juggling contest or the unicycle contest? No.

Did one of them win the tight rope contest or the trapeze contest? No.

But all the other rats agreed that the bragging rats won one contest. They were the best clowns anybody had ever seen.

"I knew I'd win," Moe said. "Because I'm the best clown in the world."

"No way," Sherlock said. "I got a lot more laughter than you did. People who know good clowns know I am really funny."

The wise old rat said, "More arguing. Here we go again."

This story is over.

grass

1. On line 1, write about what the white goat is eating.
2. On line 2, write about which goat is eating apples.

A boy loved things that fl<u>ew</u>. He loved airplanes and birds and kites and balloons. He asked his mother, "Could I be a bird so I can fly?"

His mother said, "You can not be a bird. You are a boy, and boys can't be birds."

The boy said, "But I want to fly."

"You can't fly," his mother said. "But you can fly your kite."

The boy thought flying his kite was a great plan. So he and his mother went to the park and fl<u>ew</u> his kite.

1. The boy loved things that ▬▬▬▬ .
2. The boy asked his mother if he could be a ▬▬▬▬ .
3. Could the boy become a bird?
4. What did the boy want to fly?
5. Where did the boy and his mother go to fly it?

132

1. <u>pack</u>age
2. <u>m</u>ilking
3. <u>unders</u>tand
4. <u>clothe</u>spin
5. vi<u>li</u>n
6. <u>le</u>t<u>t</u>ers

1. changed
2. space
3. dice
4. bridge
5. choice
6. pounced

1. G<u>oo</u>ber
2. p<u>o</u>rch
3. sn<u>oo</u>ze
4. ch<u>ew</u>
5. f<u>ew</u>
6. thr<u>ew</u>

1. dud
2. beet
3. dot
4. west
5. squeak
6. flake

1. int<u>erest</u>
2. <u>puppy</u>
3. <u>rocky</u>
4. <u>fatter</u>
5. <u>friendly</u>
6. <u>remembering</u>

Goober
Part One

There once were two towns, East Town and West Town. Those towns were about two miles apart. Right between the two towns was a farm. And on that farm lived a man everybody called Goober.

That wasn't really his name, but that's what they called him. Everybody knew Goober. If you asked the people who lived in East Town or West Town what they thought about Goober, you would find out that they didn't know how to feel about him. They liked him for some things, and they hated him for other things.

They liked his music. It was sweet and fine. Goober made music with an old violin. You would never know it was old from the lovely sound it made. Goober sat on his porch every summer evening and played his violin. The air would carry that pretty music for miles.

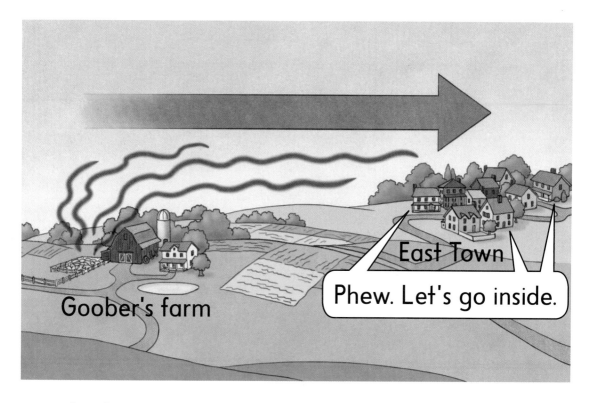

So the people in East Town and West Town would sit outside and listen to the sweet music if the wind was blowing the right way.

But if the wind was not blowing the right way, most people didn't stay outside and listen to the music. They ran inside very fast. And at those times, most people didn't like Goober. Why? Goober's farm had a very bad smell. He had dirty pigs that never took a bath. And their smell was so bad that when the wind was blowing to the east, people in East Town could smell it. Most people would say "phew" and go inside. They would close all the doors and windows—even if the evening was very warm. They would keep their houses closed up until the wind changed and stopped blowing toward East Town.

A few people would stay outside and listen to the music. Those people would put a clothespin over their nose so they could not smell anything. They would listen to the music until after the sun went down. Then they would go inside and take the clothespin off their nose.

More to come.

green

1. On line I, write about which boy wore a yellow shirt.
2. On line 2, write about what a short boy wore.

A dog loved to dig. He found a little mole hole and started to make it bigger. And as the hole got deeper and deeper, the hill of dirt next to the hole got bigger and bigger. Soon that hill was almost as big as a mountain. The dog told his pals, "I made a mountain out of a mole hill."

A mole saw the mountain and said, "This pile of dirt is too big." So the mole started putting the dirt back into the hole. The mountain got smaller and smaller until it was a tiny hill. The mole told his pals. "The dog made a mountain out of a mole hill, but I made a mole hill out of a mountain."

1. Who made a mole hole bigger?
2. Who put most of the dirt back in the hole?
3. The dog told his pals that he made a ____ out of a ____ ____.
4. The mole told his pals that he made a ____ ____ out of a ____.

A

1. bulldog
2. butterflies
3. snowflakes
4. clothespin
5. package
6. understand

B

1. dice
2. lodge
3. danger
4. strange
5. south
6. golly

C

1. tools
2. holding
3. scrubbed
4. shaped
5. smelling
6. sniffed

D

1. catch
2. lost
3. track
4. pay
5. letters

E

1. kennel
2. lets
3. plow
4. ruff
5. puppy

Goober
Part Two

Goober lived on a farm that was right between two towns. When the wind was blowing to the east, most of the people in East Town were not very happy. And when the wind was blowing to the west, most of the people in West Town were not very happy.

The people were not happy because of the smell from Goober's farm. But when they ran inside to get away from the smell, they could not hear Goober's sweet music. Some people really wanted to hear Goober's violin music. Those people stayed outside and put clothespins on their noses. But then they didn't like to talk to each other. They couldn't say words that had the letters **N** or **M**. They couldn't say the word **not**. It sounded like **dot**. They couldn't say the word **meet**. It sounded like **beet**.

The people in East Town and West Town loved it when there was no wind. Then they could all sit outside and listen to Goober's lovely violin music.

Some people liked Goober all the time. They lived more than a mile from Goober's farm. The wind would carry the smell from Goober's pigs a mile, but no more. So the smell would not reach people who lived far away. They could still hear Goober's violin and listen to the sweet music without having to smell Goober's farm.

One summer morning, something very strange happened. A little girl from West Town went over to Goober's farm to visit him. That was strange because nobody ever visited Goober.

The little girl took a package with her. She walked up to his barn. Goober was milking a cow. Stinky pigs were all around him. The little girl held her nose because the smell was very bad. She tried to say, "Mister Goober, you make nice music."

But she was holding her nose. So here is how it sounded. "Bister Goober, you bake dice busic."

Goober looked up and said, "I do what?"

She said, "Bake dice busic."

He said, "I don't understand. If you would stop holding your nose, I would know what you are trying to say."

More to come.

short

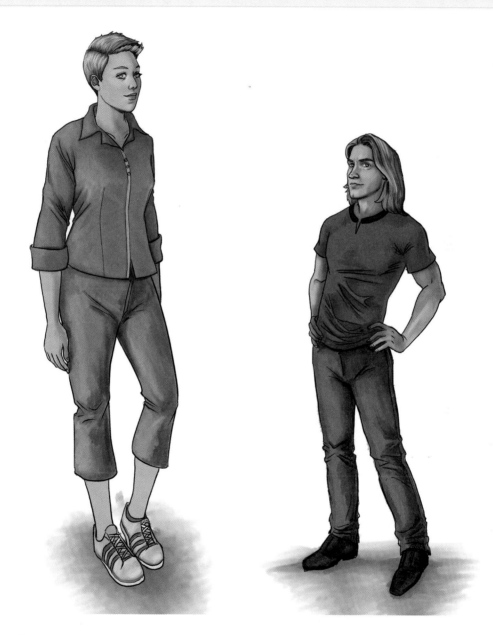

1. On line 1, write about what kind of hair the tall woman has.

2. On line 2, write about who has long hair.

Kathy liked to go to the forest and look for birds. One day, she went into the forest and heard a little tiny bird song. She said to herself, "That bird has a tiny voice, so it must be a tiny bird." She looked up in the trees and saw a tiny yellow bird.

Then she heard a great loud bird song. She said to herself, "That must be a great big bird." She looked up in the trees and all around, but she did not see a great big bird. She saw some black birds and a little tiny red bird. As she was watching the red bird, it opened its little tiny beak and let out a great loud song. Kathy said to herself, "Some birds have a little body, but a big voice."

1. Where did Kathy go to see birds?
2. One day she heard a tiny song and saw a _____ yellow bird.
3. What kind of song did she hear next?
4. A _____ _____ bird let out a great song.
5. What kind of voice do some tiny birds have?

1. ruff
2. scrubbed
3. sniffed
4. flat
5. south
6. plowed

1. waddle
2. middle
3. bulldog
4. yawned
5. noticed
6. puppy

1. life
2. track
3. ham
4. rabbit
5. golly

1. lost
2. catch
3. gone
4. wrong
5. hours

We love your music, but . . .

Goober
Part Three

A little girl went to visit Goober. She had a package with her. She tried to talk to Goober, but she was holding her nose, and he could not understand what she was trying to say. She tried to say, "You make nice music," but she really said, "You bake dice busic." Goober told her to stop holding her nose so he could understand what she was saying.

So the little girl took in a lot of air. Then she let go of her nose and talked very quickly. She said, "We love your music, but you need to clean up your pigs. They stink." When she was done talking, she grabbed her nose again.

Goober's eyes got wide. He looked at the little girl for a long time. Then he said, "Do my pigs really stink?"

She said, "Yes."

"Golly," he said. "I didn't know that."

She handed Goober her package and said, "Here are sub thigs for you." She turned around and ran away. She was still holding her nose.

Goober opened the package. Inside were some bars of pig soap.

Goober smelled the soap and said, "What a strange smell."

Then Goober went down to the pond with the package. He called his pigs. They came running. Then he jumped into the pond with the pigs and scrubbed them until they were pink. Scrub, scrub, scrub. He rubbed and scrubbed and washed and cleaned. When he was done, his pigs were as clean and sweet smelling as anybody in East Town or West Town. He sniffed the air and said, "These pigs really smell strange."

Now things are different in West Town and East Town. Everybody sits outside and listens to the music each summer evening. No matter which way the wind blows, the air is as sweet as the violin music they listen to. If you go to one of those towns and ask people about Goober, they'll have wonderful things to say about him and his music. And they also have some very nice things to say about a little girl from West Town who goes to visit Goober every week. She always leaves a package with him, and the people in West Town and East Town are very glad that she does.

The end.

1. On line 1, write about what a man will carry.
2. On line 2, write about who will carry a green bag.

Marta didn't like to get dirty, but she wanted to help her mom plant some trees in their yard. She put on her mittens so her hands wouldn't get dirty. She put on her old pants too. She didn't want to get her nice school pants dirty.

When Marta went outside to help, Marta's mom was very dirty from planting trees. Her hands were dirty, and her shirt was dirty. There was also dirt in her hair.

Marta and her mom watered the plants and patted the dirt around the plants. Marta got mud all over her mittens. When she rubbed her fa<u>ce</u>, she got dirt all over it. Pretty soon, Marta was as dirty as her mom and had dirt everywhere. Marta didn't mind. She said, "Sometimes getting dirty is fun."

1. What did Marta want to help her mom do?

2. Marta put on mittens to keep her hands from getting ███ .

3. Did Marta's mom get dirty?

4. Marta and her mom ended up with dirt ███ .

5. Marta said, "Sometimes getting dirty is ███ ."

1. Andrea
2. Honey
3. waddled
4. life
5. middle
6. butterflies

1. alarm
2. napping
3. swung
4. hissed
5. net
6. snort

1. nip
2. snip
3. flew
4. threw
5. snakes
6. flakes

1. ski
2. interesting
3. cloth
4. clothes
5. often
6. station

Honey and Sweetie
Part One

There once was the meanest looking bulldog you ever saw. Her bottom teeth stuck out, and she looked like she was ready to bite somebody. People were always shocked to find out that this bulldog was named Honey.

She got that name because she was as sweet as honey. She loved people. She loved other dogs. She even liked some animals you would not think a dog would like. One of Honey's friends was a little gray mouse named Andrea.

Honey would sometimes sniff around the house trying to find Andrea. Andrea lived in the hall. She really lived behind a little hole in the hall wall. But in the middle of the day, she could be in a lot of places. So Honey would sniff around and try to find her. Sometimes Honey would find Andrea, and sometimes she wouldn't, because Andrea was very, very shy.

There was only one thing that Honey didn't like. That was cats. She could get along with some cats. But she really didn't like cats that chased birds, butterflies, or mice. She said to herself, "That's not nice."

One day, Honey was napping on the back porch of her house. She woke up when a woman holding a big yellow cat named Sweetie came up the steps. When Honey saw that cat, she said to herself, "Yuk. I hope that thing does not stay around here very long."

The woman and her cat Sweetie went inside. After a while, Honey got up, yawned, and waddled into the house.

The woman was sitting at the table in the kitchen, but where was the cat? That's what the woman wanted to know too. She said, "Where did Sweetie go?"

Everybody found out where he was in the next moment. The sounds of running came from the next room. Honey waddled quickly into that room. When Honey saw what was happening, she became very mad. Poor little Andrea was running for her life. And right behind her was that mean yellow cat. The cat and the mouse shot around the room, this way and that way. They went under the table and across the rug. Then they went into the hall, around a coat stand, and back to the room where Honey was standing.

More next time.

small   pink

1. On line 1, write about what a tan rabbit eats off of.
2. On line 2, write about what kind of bug eats off of a big plate.

Sammy the goat liked to go for walks. Sammy never got tired of walking.

One day, Sammy wanted to walk to the forest. That forest was very far away. He told the other goats, "I'm going to walk all the way to the forest, and I'm going alone."

"No, don't go alone," the other goats said. "It's too far."

Sammy didn't listen to those goats. So he walked for miles and miles. Pretty soon, it was getting dark, and Sammy still wasn't at the forest. He was starting to get scared.

This is not the end.

1. What did Sammy like to do?
2. Where did Sammy want to walk to?
3. Was the forest near the farm?
4. Did his goat friends think he should go alone?
5. It was getting dark and Sammy was starting to get ▮▮▮▮▮.

136

A
1. ski
2. cloth
3. often
4. station
5. waddled
6. answer

B
1. scraps
2. thick
3. nip
4. given
5. hissed
6. howled

C
1. soup
2. slopes
3. ruff
4. meat
5. net
6. swung

D
1. interesting
2. kennel
3. snorting
4. sticking
5. shouldn't
6. what's

E
1. bend
2. scales
3. tip
4. wife
5. fit
6. neck

Honey and Sweetie
Part Two

Poor little Andrea was being chased by a mean yellow cat named Sweetie. They had run down the hall and back into the room where Honey was standing. Honey was ready to help Andrea out, but before she could do anything, Andrea and Sweetie darted under the table again. Sweetie tried to pounce on Andrea, but his claws got stuck on the table cloth. Down came the table cloth. It fell over Sweetie like a big white net.

It's time to teach you a lesson.

Sweetie tried to get free. He swung at the table cloth, bit at it, and tried to roll away from it. But the more he tried to fight and roll, the more he was trapped inside that table cloth. Only two parts of Sweetie were sticking out. His yellow tail was sticking out of one end of the table cloth, and his nose was sticking out of the other end.

While Sweetie was rolling around and trying to get free, Andrea darted down the hall and into her hole. She was very scared. Honey looked at Sweetie and said to herself, "It is time to teach this cat a lesson."

She waddled over to Sweetie and gave his tail a little bite. It was not a great bite, just a little nip. "There," Honey said to herself, and waddled outside.

To Sweetie, Honey's little nip felt like a great bite.
Sweetie howled and hissed and rolled around inside the
table cloth. At last, he got free. He looked around the
room, but he didn't see Andrea because she was in her
mouse hole. And Sweetie didn't see Honey because she
was outside. Sweetie didn't know who bit his tail. He
never saw Honey in the room, so he didn't even think
about her. He said to himself, "The only one who could
have given me that big bite was that little tiny mouse."

Sweetie shook his head and said to himself, "How
can that mouse look really weak, but have such a
hard bite?"

That was the last time Sweetie ever chased
Andrea. In fact, there are a lot of things that Sweetie
does not chase. He doesn't chase mice, and he
doesn't try to grab little birds.

The end.

1. On line 1, write about what the woman gathered.

2. On line 2, write about who gathered green apples.

Sammy the goat had been walking for a very long time, and it was getting dark. Sammy was scared to be alone in the dark. He stopped near a stream and said, "I wish my friends were here." Then he said, "I will rest here. I hope no lions or tigers come after me."

Just as he was falling asleep, he heard loud noises. The noises were coming closer and closer. Sammy was very afraid. But then, he saw it. It was his goat friends.

Sammy's fear turned to joy. One of his pals shouted. "Sammy, we couldn't let you go by yourself. We wanted to make sure you were safe."

The goats slept next to the stream that night. The next day, Sammy and his pals walked to the forest together and made it back home that evening.

The end.

1. Was Sammy afraid to be alone in the dark?
2. Where did Sammy stop and rest?
3. Who did Sammy hear coming closer and closer?
4. What did Sammy's fear turn into?
5. Before going home, where did Sammy and his pals walk?

137

1. often
2. gone
3. wrong
4. lost

1. h<u>ou</u>rs
2. cat<u>ch</u>
3. al<u>ar</u>m
4. sn<u>or</u>ting
5. hunt<u>er</u>s
6. mirr<u>or</u>

1. <u>chasing</u>
2. <u>finding</u>
3. <u>tracking</u>
4. <u>picking</u>
5. <u>acting</u>
6. <u>boring</u>
7. <u>snoring</u>

1. clim<u>b</u>ers
2. snowballs
3. rabbit
4. dan<u>g</u>er
5. station
6. minutes

1. Dud
2. ham
3. slope
4. flat
5. either
6. scraps

Dot and Dud
Part One

Once there were two big work dogs named Dot and Dud. Dot was Dud's sister. The two dogs lived with five other work dogs at the ranger station high in the mountains. The job of the dogs was to find mountain climbers and hikers who got lost or hurt. That was their job, but there was one big problem with that job. That problem was Dud. They called him Dud because that's what he was—a big dud at doing his job. When a climber was missing, the ranger would send the dogs to find him. The other dogs would find the climber. Then they would have to find Dud. Dud would get lost. Most of the time, the dog who found the mountain climber was Dot. She was the best dog at finding people lost in the mountains.

Dud was not good at his job because he didn't like to work. He didn't like to put his nose in the cold snow and sniff for a smell that would lead him to the lost person. Dud acted like he was tracking through the snow, but he was just acting. While he should have been thinking about finding the lost climber, he was often thinking about eating a large ham bone or sleeping next to the big fire place down at the ranger station.

Most of the other work dogs would get mad at Dud because they knew he wasn't trying hard. "Come on," they'd say to him. "Stop being such a baby and get to work."

"Okay," Dud would say. "I will. I will." But he didn't.

One time, the other dogs got really mad. Dud had gone out to find a climber, but he got lost. The other dogs spent hours looking for him. After they found Dud and got back to the kennel, the oldest dog said, "While we work, you are out there playing around, running after your tail, rolling snowballs with your nose, or chasing rabbits."

"Yeah," another dog said. "And you don't even know where you are. When we found you, you were less than a mile from the station, and you didn't even know how to get back here."

Dot said, "Stop picking on my brother. He can do this job, and he will work hard. Won't you, Dud?"

"I will. I will," Dud said. "I'll work hard."

Dud was not telling a lie. He had made up his mind to do a good job. But of course, the other dogs didn't believe him.

More next time.

she small

1. On line 1, write about what kind of tracks he saw in the snow.

2. On line 2, write about who saw big tracks in the mud.

A black eagle lived near a stream. One day that eagle was in a tree when she saw a big fish. She said, "That fish is near a large brown rock. So I will swoop down and go right over that rock. Then I will grab that fish out of the water."

The eagle swooped down, but her plan didn't work, because the brown rock mov<u>e</u>d. And she fl<u>ew</u> right into it. That brown rock was not a rock at all. It was a moose. And the moose was very mad at the eagle.

So now the eagle makes sure there are no big brown rocks in the stream before she swoops down to go fishing.

1. What kind of bird wanted to get a fish?

2. Was the eagle red, black, or yellow?

3. The eagle planned to swoop over a large ▮▮▮▮ ▮▮▮▮.

4. The brown rock was really a ▮▮▮▮.

5. How did the moose feel after the eagle fl<u>ew</u> into it?

138

1. sure
2. ski
3. soup
4. wrong
5. dan<u>ge</u>r
6. polite

1. <u>popular</u>
2. <u>headed</u>
3. <u>snowing</u>
4. <u>snoozing</u>
5. <u>snowflak</u>es
6. <u>noisy</u>

1. <u>slope</u>s
2. <u>reached</u>
3. <u>barked</u>
4. <u>nights</u>
5. <u>rocky</u>
6. <u>wise</u>r

1. ex<u>cept</u>
2. <u>clinic</u>
3. <u>trouble</u>
4. <u>problems</u>

1. fit
2. thick
3. lo<u>dge</u>
4. scraps
5. passed
6. sid<u>es</u>

Dot and Dud

Part Two

The other work dogs were mad at Dud for being a dud. Dud was also mad at himself. He had made up his mind to try harder. That's what he told the others, but they didn't believe him. He had said the same thing many times before.

Just then, the alarm sounded. That told the dogs that a mountain climber was in danger. Three rangers ran to the kennel and let the dogs out. The dogs left the station and headed north to where mountain climbers climb. The dogs sniffed for the trail of the lost climber as they went up higher and higher. At first, Dud tried his best. Dud put his nose in the snow a few times and tried very hard to smell something. He was working hard, sniffing and snorting and going up the steep slope.

After a while, Dud began to walk slower and slower.

Dot was leading the way up the mountain. Dot looked back and saw Dud falling behind. "Come on, Dud!" she shouted. "You can do it. Keep working hard." But Dud kept walking slower and falling farther behind, and Dot kept tracking the lost climber.

Then Dud came to a place that was not steep. It was almost flat. There, Dud did something that was more interesting than sniffing snow. He chased his shadow. Dud jumped up, and the shadow moved. Dud pounced on the shadow. He rolled over the shadow. He ran around and around, faster and faster, trying to catch that shadow. He even barked at his shadow. This was fun, fun, fun.

Right in the middle of the game, the shadow went away. Dud looked up and saw clouds in the sky. Now it was snowing. Dud couldn't see any of the other dogs. He knew that they were heading north, but he had been running around so much that he didn't know which way north was. He knew that he had to go up a slope, but there were a lot of slopes. Which slope was the right one?

Soon the snow was coming down so hard that Dud couldn't see any slopes—only snow, snow, snow.

Dud looked this way and that way. He tried to sniff the air, but all he could smell were snowflakes. At last he made a choice about which way to go, and his choice was wrong, wrong, wrong. Poor Dud started heading south, not north. He was heading right back toward the ranger station.

More next time.

plate   cup

1. On line 1, write about what is on a table with corners.

2. On line 2, write about what is on a round table.

162

Little Billy loved to go shopping. One day he was with his mom at a mall. He said, "Today, I'm going to go shopping by myself." So Billy left his mother and went into a big store. That store had everything. Little Billy got a cart and loaded it with shoes, coats, <u>too</u>ls, food, books, and just about anything else he could reach. Then Billy started to roll the cart with his things out of the store. A big man stopped him and said, "You have to pay for these things."

Little Billy looked up at the man and said, "Pay? I don't know how to pay."

Just then Billy's mom ran into the store. She said, "I'm sorry for what happened. Little Billy sometimes forgets that he is just three years old."

1. What did Billy like to do?

2. Name two things he put in his cart.

3. Before Billy could take his things out of the store, what did he have to do with them?

4. What kind of man stopped Billy?

5. How old was Billy?

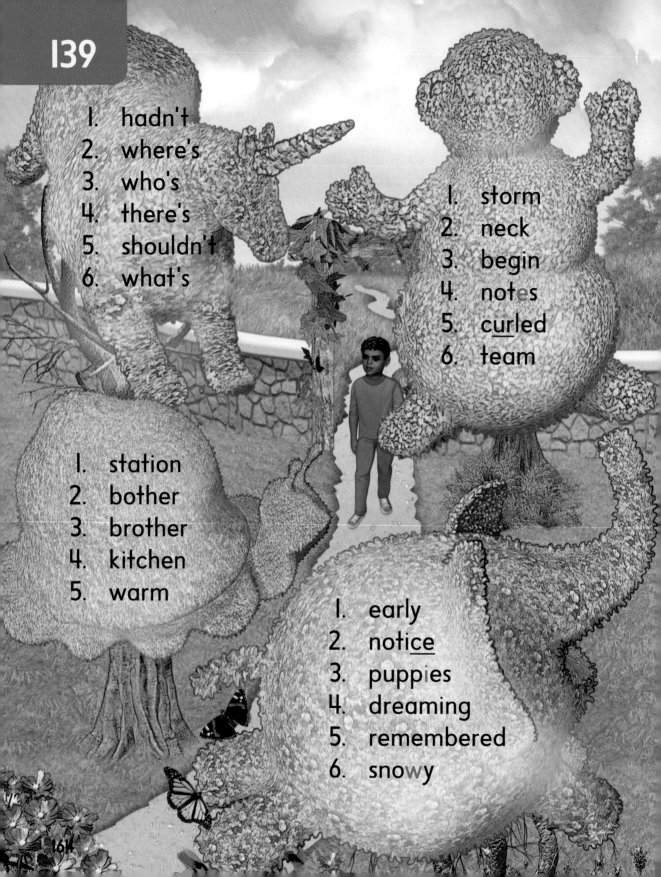

1. hadn't
2. where's
3. who's
4. there's
5. shouldn't
6. what's

1. storm
2. neck
3. begin
4. notes
5. curled
6. team

1. station
2. bother
3. brother
4. kitchen
5. warm

1. early
2. notice
3. puppies
4. dreaming
5. remembered
6. snowy

Dot and Dud
Part Three

Dud was trying to go north, but he went south. He went very close to the ranger station. But he didn't see it and went right on past it. The snow was coming down so hard that he couldn't see the station, and he was so lazy that he didn't bother sniffing with his nose. So Dud passed that station and went up a mountain to the south of the station. At last he came to a large ski lodge where there were many people.

Dud did not know where he was, but he said to himself, "There are people here, so there must be a kitchen around here." Dud found the kitchen very quickly by sniffing for the smells of ham and eggs.

Then Dud put on a little act. He sat outside the kitchen and made little barks. "Ruff, ruff." When a woman opened the door, he wagged his tail and tried to look very friendly, but also very cold.

"What are you doing out here?" the woman said. "You poor dog. You must be very hungry and tired. Come in here."

She led Dud inside and gave him a lot of soup and a big pile of meat scraps. This was like a dream for Dud. He ate everything and then took a wonderful nap right next to the big, warm stove. He was one happy dog.

But while he was snoozing, things were not going well for the other dogs. Dot had found the trail of the lost mountain climber, but in the snow storm, the other dogs could not keep up with her. She followed the trail up slopes that were so steep that she kept slipping. Once she slipped and slid down a long way. Dot got up and kept trying until she reached a rocky place where the mountain climber was sitting. He was hurt and couldn't walk. He just sat there with his eyes closed. Dot knew that he was in bad shape.

She barked and howled to let the other dogs know she had found the climber. The other dogs were over a mile away and couldn't hear anything because of the howling winds and thick falling snow. Dot had to stay with the climber, so she curled up next to him to keep him warm. Then she waited, and waited, and waited. It was getting close to night time.

More to come.

short	green

1. On line 1, write about what kind of toad is on a long stick.

2. On line 2, write about what kind of stick a brown toad is on.

Not all fish in the sea look the same. You can often tell where a fish lives by the shape of the fish. Fish that live near the shore are shaped like this. The shape of these fish lets them turn quickly.

Fish that live far from shore look like this. The shape of these fish lets them swim very fast.

Some fish that live in the open water far from shore hunt other fish. The fish that hunt have to be fast. Sometimes hunting fish come near the shore and hunt those round shaped fish. The round shaped fish that live near the shore are good at getting away from the hunting fish.

1. Do all fish that live in the sea have the same shape?

2. Round shaped fish often live near the ▅▅▅▅.

3. Do fast swimming fish that hunt often live near the shore?

4. What can round shaped fish do very quickly?

1. practice
2. tomorrow
3. begin
4. finish
5. changing
6. somewhere

1. station
2. nation
3. question
4. action
5. motion

1. team
2. point
3. mast
4. voices
5. melts
6. added

1. early
2. knowing
3. noticed
4. slight
5. quietly
6. quickly

Dot and Dud
Part Four

That evening, while Dud was sleeping in the kitchen and dreaming of summer time, a truck pulled up to the ski lodge. The head ranger came inside to pick up Dud. The cook had called the ranger station and told them that one of their dogs was at the lodge.

The ranger was not happy. He led Dud to the truck and put him in the back with the other work dogs. They were coming back from the North Mountains. They had not found the mountain climber, and they hadn't found Dot. The ranger wanted to come home before it got too dark. He planned to go out again early in the morning.

When Dud got in the truck, he didn't know that Dot was lost on the mountain. But right away, he knew that something was wrong. The other dogs didn't start complaining about Dud getting lost. Those dogs didn't even look at him. They just looked down at the floor.

172

Dud tried to talk to the other dogs. "Did you find the mountain climber?" he asked. The other dogs didn't say a thing. They just looked down.

Dud said, "You know, I had some wonderful soup at the ski lodge, and I . . ."

"Be quiet," the oldest dog said.

Dud was quiet for a while. Then he noticed that Dot was not in the truck. "Where's Dot?" he asked.

"Lost," one of the work dogs said.

"What do you mean?" Dud asked. "Where is she?"

"Somewhere on the mountain," the oldest dog said.

"Do you mean she's out there alone?"

Some of the dogs said, "Yes," very quietly.

173

Dud loved Dot. He didn't always show it, but he loved her. As he sat in the back of that truck, he remembered her from way back, when Dot and Dud were little puppies. When any other puppy would pick on Dud, Dot always stuck up for him. Dud remembered a lot of other things as the truck went down that snowy road. He remembered how sad he had been when he and Dot had to leave their mother. The only good thing about going to the ranger station was that Dot was with him.

More to come.

big	small

1. On line 1, write about which cloud rain drops fell from.

2. On line 2, write about which cloud snowflakes fell from.

Once there was a rabbit who always bragged about how fast she was. One day, when the rabbit was bragging, a little mole said, "I will race you."

The rabbit laughed and laughed. "I will race you any time," the rabbit said.

"Fine," the mole said. "Be here at one o'clock at night. And if you do not win the race, you will stop bragging."

The rabbit agreed.

That night, the rabbit and the mole were ready to start the race. Many other animals were there to watch the race, too, but it was so dark that most of the animals couldn't see. The mole said, "Ready, set, go," and both animals started to run.

Did the rabbit win the race? No. She didn't even get to the end of the race, because she couldn't see. She ran into a rock. She heard bells and saw stars. Now she doesn't brag.

1. What kind of animal bragged?
2. Who said he would race the rabbit?
3. When did the race start?
4. Why didn't the rabbit win?
5. Does the rabbit brag any more?

142

1. vacation
2. mention
3. action
4. nation

1. guy
2. doctor
3. clinic
4. question
5. practiced
6. finish

1. trouble
2. slight
3. cools
4. tomorrow
5. talks
6. mold

1. lowered
2. swimmers
3. licked
4. darkness
5. plowing
6. peas

If they can't find her, I will.

Dot and Dud
Part Five

Dud was in the back of the ranger's truck, remembering how much he loved Dot. All at once, he said, "No, she can't be lost." Then he turned to the oldest dog and asked, "Why did you leave her out there?"

"She'll be all right if we find her early in the morning."

Dud said, "But what about the mountain climber? Won't he freeze if he stays out there much longer?"

All the other dogs looked down.

Dud didn't say anything more to the other dogs. But he said something to himself. He said, "If they can't find her, I'll find her." Dud was not talking the way he sometimes did when he said, "I'll work harder." This time Dud was not just saying something he thought the other dogs wanted to hear. Dud was going to find Dot.

178

The truck stopped in front of the ranger station. As soon as the ranger opened the back door, Dud jumped out and darted away as fast as he could. The ranger shouted, "Dud, come back here. It's dark out there."

The other dogs barked and yelled, "Come back you lazy dog. You don't know where you are going."

Dud knew where he was going—north, to find Dot.

I will find her. I will.

Pretty soon some of the other dogs started to follow Dud. Then all of them followed. Then the ranger followed. Away they went, plowing through the deep snow up the mountain. Dud said to himself, "I know Dot's smell better than anyone else's in the world. I will find that smell. I will. I will."

He put his nose in the snow and snorted and sniffed. He didn't even notice that the snow was cold. Again and again—snort, sniff, snort, sniff. Then he did it the fast way. He just put his nose in the snow and kept it there, running up the slopes like a snow plow, snorting and sniffing. And up the mountain he went, just as fast as he could run.

Suddenly, there was a very slight smell in the snow. It was Dot. Yes, yes, yes. It was Dot. "Come on," Dud barked to the other dogs. "Follow me."

And up the mountain he went once more, his head in the snow like a snow plow. When he came to steep parts and slid down, he just tried harder and did it again until he made it. Her smell was getting stronger and stronger. Dud and the other dogs knew that Dud was leading them closer and closer to Dot and the climber.

More to come.

horse

1. On line 1, write about what a black car is behind.

2. On line 2, write about what is behind a red car.

Jim was a snake that loved to eat bugs. One year, there were lots of bugs, and Jim ate, and ate, and ate. But the more he ate, the fatter he got. Soon he was so fat that he could not sneak up on bugs. He couldn't slide through the grass. He plowed through the grass. The bugs would hear him coming and call to each other, "Here comes that fat snake again. Let's get out of here."

And they would.

Jim has not had a bug to eat in two weeks. Now he is not as fat so he can slide through the grass better than before. But he won't be able to catch bugs for another week.

1. What kind of animal was Jim?
2. What did he love to eat?
3. What happened to Jim after he ate and ate?
4. Could he sneak up on bugs anymore?
5. How long will it be before he is able to catch bugs?

143

1. direct
2. direc<u>tion</u>
3. inform
4. informa<u>tion</u>
5. collect
6. collec<u>tion</u>

1. <u>bor</u>ing
2. <u>snor</u>ing
3. <u>will</u>ing
4. <u>plant</u>ed
5. <u>drift</u>ed
6. <u>dark</u>ness

1. wif<u>e</u>
2. popular
3. regular
4. low<u>er</u>ed
5. doctor
6. licked

1. glass
2. bottle
3. swerve
4. elevator
5. either

1. through
2. thought
3. minutes
4. except
5. tomorrow

Dot and Dud
Part Six

Dud was leading the other dogs high into the North Mountains. He knew that he was getting very close to Dot because her smell was strong.

Suddenly Dud stopped and looked up. He had come to the rocky part where Dot was curled up next to the mountain climber. For a moment, Dud stood there and looked into the darkness. He could see Dot. He ran over, sat down next to her, and licked her nose. "Are you okay?" he asked.

"Yes," she said. "But I'm so glad you're here. I don't think the mountain climber could make it through the night in this cold."

Dot and Dud looked at each other and wagged their tails. Then Dud called to the other dogs, "Come up here. I found them."

The ranger used ropes and poles to make it up the rocky part with the other dogs. The ranger had a little sled. With care, he put the climber on the sled. The ranger and the dogs used ropes to lower the sled down the very steep parts. The dogs took the sled down the rest of the mountain. Even in the darkness, the dogs and ranger took the sled down the mountain quickly.

After the ranger took the mountain climber to a doctor, he went back to the ranger station and put the dogs in the kennel.

This bone is for you.

The dogs were very tired and curled up in their beds right away. Dud was starting to fall asleep when the oldest dog said, "I want to thank Dud for finding Dot and saving a mountain climber."

All the other dogs looked up and waited for the oldest dog to finish. "Dud showed what he can do when he really puts his mind to it. I know now that he's going to be pretty good at his job."

The other dogs nodded their heads.

Just then, the ranger thanked the dogs by leaving a pile of meat scraps and a large ham bone. The oldest dog picked up the ham bone and took it over to Dud. He said, "This is for you."

Dud picked up the ham bone and took it to Dot. "You are the best dog. I did tonight what you do every day. I will work hard to some day be as good at saving people as you are."

The other dogs cheered.

From that day on, Dud worked hard and helped save many other hikers and climbers.

The end.

1. On line 1, write about how many people fl<u>ew</u> in a short plane.

2. On line 2, write about what three people fl<u>ew</u> in.

Sharks are hunters of the sea. Sharks are fish, and they are very strong. Sharks do not have teeth or bones like yours. The teeth of sharks are really just scales. The bones of sharks are not like your bones.

Your bones are very hard and do not bend. Shark bones bend and are not made of the same material your bones are made of.

Your bones hold up the part of your nose near your face. Grab your nose near your face, just below your eyes. Try to move the base of your nose from side to side. Your bones do not bend.

A shark's bones are made of what holds up the tip of your nose. Grab the tip of your nose and move it from side to side. Shark bones bend just like that.

1. Are sharks fish?

2. The teeth of the shark are really ▇▇▇▇ .

3. A shark's bones are made of the same things that hold up the tip of your ▇▇▇▇ .

4. Do your bones bend?

5. Do a shark's bones bend?

144

1. polite
2. snoring
3. boring
4. either
5. except
6. melted

1. patient
2. certain
3. clinic
4. practice
5. trouble

1. area
2. Bill Wilson
3. Milly
4. minute
5. experts
6. asleep

1. popular
2. school
3. sure
4. wife
5. answer

1. ago
2. giant
3. islands
4. finger
5. bothered
6. master

Boring Bill
Part One

Bill Wilson was a nice man. He was kind to dogs, cats, and other animals. He took good care of his car, his house, and his lawn. He loved his wife, Milly, and he liked people. He was always willing to help people when they needed help, and he was very polite.

Bill Wilson did all of these nice things, but he still was not a very popular person. You see, Bill was boring. He was so boring that every time he started talking, he would put people to sleep. Within a few minutes, people would either be yawning or leaving the room. Within a few more minutes, anybody who stayed in the room would be snoring.

Bill once gave a talk to parents at a school. After only ten minutes, everybody except Bill was asleep. The room was very noisy because people were snoring so loudly. After the meeting, one woman said, "We were snoring because Bill is boring." From that day on, people called Bill Wilson "Boring Bill." They didn't say it to his face, but they said it. And Bill knew about it.

One evening, Bill said to his wife, "The more I speak, the more people sleep. There must be something I can do to be less boring, but I'm not sure what different things I can do. Tell me, Milly, what should I do to be less boring?"

Milly didn't answer him, because she was sound asleep. Bill looked at her and said to himself, "I must do something to change the way I talk. I am tired of being so boring."

More to come.

small short

1. On line 1, write about what the tiger with big ears is on.

2. On line 2, write about which tiger is on the tall ladder.

Jen liked to make things, but the things she made didn't fit. Once she made a hat for her brother. That hat went over his ears, his eyes, his nose, his mouth, and his neck. He said, "This hat is so big, it could be a bag."

He cut three holes in it. One hole was on top. The other two holes were on the sides. He gave the hat to a little girl and said, "Here is a fine dress for you."

She loved that dress and looked really good in it too. It fit her very well.

1. Who liked to make things?

2. Did the things she made fit well?

3. What did she try to make for her brother?

4. He made it into something for a little girl. What was that?

5. How did it fit the little girl?

145

1. babies
2. stories
3. ladies

4. baby
5. story
6. lady

1. amazing
2. young
3. questions
4. speaking
5. moves
6. mirror

1. rang
2. bounce
3. blub

4. piece
5. pea
6. root

1. finished
2. normal
3. difference
4. changes
5. certainly
6. practicing

1. explaining
2. interest
3. wasting
4. beauty
5. paddle
6. beetle

Boring Bill
Part Two

Bill tried to say things that would interest other people. He asked questions and tried to get people to talk about themselves. He tried to say things that were funny. He tried to talk faster and louder. He tried to smile more when he talked. But all those changes made no difference. After Bill was through speaking, everybody else was sleeping.

One day, Bill was at home. In front of the mirror, he was practicing being less boring. He smiled, moved around a lot, and talked to the mirror.

Just then the door bell rang. Bill opened the door and saw a woman who said, "I am an expert at making people sleep. I work for the Sleep More Clinic. We help people who have trouble sleeping. I hear that you can make people sleep, too."

"Yes," Bill said. "If I speak for a while, people will sleep."

"That is interesting," the sleep expert said.
"Can you explain how you make people sleep?"

"Yes, I can." Bill said. "It seems that I am
boring." Bill went on to explain why he was boring
and tell about some things that happened to him.
When Bill finished explaining his problem, he
noticed that the sleep expert was snoring.

They won't fall asleep.

Bill woke the expert up. The expert said, "Oh, dear. I don't know what came over me. I was listening to what you said, and then . . ."

Bill said, "Oh, I understand. That happens to me all the time."

The expert said, "Do you mind if I come back tomorrow with some other experts from the clinic?"

"No, I don't mind."

After the expert left, Bill made up his mind that he would be interesting when the others visited him. He said to himself, "Tomorrow, I will talk in a way that the experts will not be able to fall asleep."

More to come.

small   white

1. On line I, write about which dog has a big feather.

2. On line 2, write about what kind of feather the brown dog has.

I have four legs, two arms, and a back. I stand about four feet high, and almost all of me is made of wood. My legs do not bend, and they hold me up.

I have a soft seat where people can sit. People rest their arms on my arms and their backs on my back. I will stay where you put me, but I don't like to be left alone for a long time. Please sit on me.

1. Do the legs bend?
2. Name the part that is soft.
3. What do people do with this thing?
4. What kind of thing is telling this story?

car   chair   dog

146

1. mold
2. paddle
3. paper
4. river
5. beetles
6. root

1. stories
2. babies
3. ponies
4. parties

1. thirty
2. twenty
3. bottle
4. finger
5. message
6. write

1. amazing
2. honking
3. bouncing
4. lifting
5. keeping
6. hitting

1. young
2. guy
3. bear
4. patients
5. certain
6. certainly

203

Boring Bill
Part Three

Nine experts from the Sleep More Clinic were on their way to visit Bill. One of them kept arguing with the others. She said, "I don't believe those stories about how Bill is able to make people sleep. We know more about putting people to sleep than he knows. After all, we are experts. Bill is not an expert, so Bill can't know more about sleep than we know. I think we are wasting our time."

The woman who visited Bill the day before said, "We are not wasting our time."

The leader of the team said, "Now, now. Let's not argue. We'll listen to what Bill has to say. I want everybody to take notes and ask good questions."

When they got to Bill's place, they asked Bill to explain how he put people to sleep. Bill said, "When I talk in my normal voice, people just fall asleep. But today, I'm talking in a voice that will keep all of you wide awake. I have been working on this voice, and it is very interesting. It is not like my normal voice, which is soft and easy. This voice has a lot of bounce. I think you'll see that . . . "

One of the experts said, "Zzzz."

Another expert said, "Snort, blub, zzzz."

The woman who believed that she knew more about putting people to sleep than Bill did said, "Gl gl honk zzzzzzzz."

Let's begin the meeting.

Bill stopped talking and waited many minutes for the others to wake up. The first one to wake up was the leader. "Oh my," he said as he looked at the others. "That was amazing. You certainly do know how to put people to sleep."

After a while, all the experts except one were awake. The only one who kept on honking and snoring was the expert who thought she knew more about putting people to sleep than Bill did.

She woke up when the experts were getting ready to leave. She said, "Well, let's begin the meeting."

The leader said, "We're through meeting. You slept through all but the start of it."

More next time.

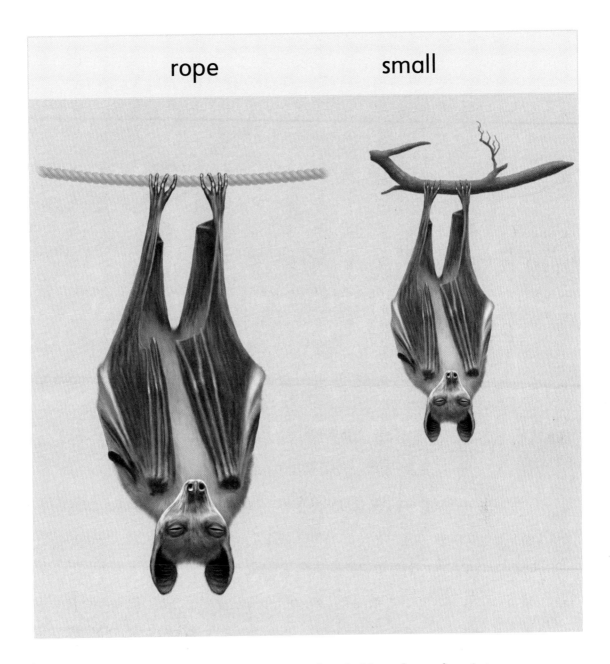

rope   small

1. On line 1, write about what the big bat is hanging from.

2. On line 2, write about which bat is hanging from a stick.

There once was a large block of ice that didn't like the cold. That ice was in a big freezer. One day, the ice said, "I'm tired of being cold. I will go where it is warm."

The other smaller blocks of ice said, "But if you go where it is warm, you will melt and turn into a puddle of water."

But the large block didn't listen to the others. That block of ice left the freezer. Soon the block noticed that it had started to melt and was getting smaller. The block of ice said, "I must go back to the freezer before I become a puddle." That block made it back to the freezer. Now the block does not hate the cold. It says, "I am smaller but wiser."

1. At first, what didn't the large block of ice like?

2. What did that block of ice live in?

3. What did the other blocks say the large block would turn into if it left?

4. After the large block left the freezer, it was getting ▮▮▮ .

5. Did that block return to the freezer?

147

1. action
2. fraction
3. fashion
4. mansion

1. buy
2. guy
3. bother
4. father
5. hairs
6. bears

1. imagine
2. build
3. nine-thirty
4. doctors
5. patients
6. area

1. swerve
2. bottle
3. ditch
4. fingers
5. master
6. message

1. elevator
2. regular
3. twenty
4. young
5. faces

Boring Bill
Part Four

When the nine experts from the Sleep More Clinic left Bill's place, he felt very sad. He had tried to be interesting, but his plan had not worked.

Later that day, Bill felt a lot better because he got a call from the leader of the expert team. The leader said, "Bill, could you come to the Sleep More Clinic tomorrow? You may be able to help us with some people who we have not been able to help sleep."

So the next morning at nine-thirty, Bill was at the Sleep More Clinic. The leader told Bill that the first patient he would see had not been able to sleep for three nights. When that patient came in, she said, "Nobody can help me sleep. What's the point of talking to another doctor? I know I won't sleep tonight either."

Bill said, "I'm not a doctor. I'm just a boring kind of guy."

The patient said, "So now I don't even get to talk to a doctor."

Bill said, "Well, you don't really have to talk. All you have to do is listen to what I say. I'll talk for a while, and before you know . . . "

"Snort. Zzzz."

The same thing happened with the next patient, a young woman who had not been able to sleep for nearly a week.

After Bill put the second patient to sleep, the leader said, "Why are we working with patients one at a time? Let's bring in all the other patients and see what happens."

So doctors brought twenty patients in. Bill talked to them for five minutes, and the room was filled with the sounds of people snorting, snoring, honking, and making lots of Zs. The sounds came from twenty patients with sleep problems and four doctors from the Sleep More Clinic who had been watching Bill work.

Before Bill left, the leader of the sleep team asked Bill, "Would you like to work at our clinic?"

We'll find out more next time.

black

1. On line 1, write about what kind of bell the small rabbit rang.

2. On line 2, write about which rabbit rang a red bell.

Steve wanted to climb a mountain. He didn't know which trail to take, but he was afraid to ask anyone. He didn't want people to think he wasn't smart. So he didn't ask any <u>qu</u>estions.

Steve went to where lots of folks hiked. He picked a trail and started up it. Soon the trail became steep and rocky. Before Steve knew it, he was standing on the <u>edge</u> of a hundred foot drop off. Steve could not turn around. He was stuck. So a ranger had to come with ropes to pull Steve off the <u>edge</u> of the drop off.

The ranger asked, "Why did you take that trail?" Steve didn't know what to say.

Later, Steve told himself, "Next time, if I don't know something, I'll ask <u>qu</u>estions about it."

1. What did Steve want to climb?

2. Did Steve know which trail to take?

3. Steve got stuck on the <u>edge</u> of a ▮▮▮ ▮▮▮ .

4. Who saved Steve?

5. Will Steve ask <u>qu</u>estions next time?

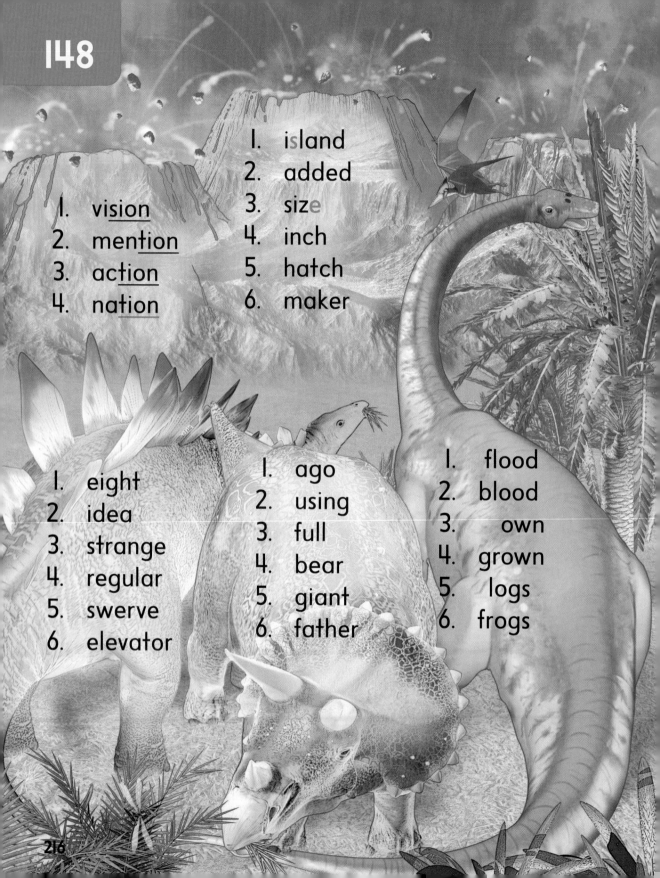

148

1. island
2. added
3. size
4. inch
5. hatch
6. maker

1. vision
2. mention
3. action
4. nation

1. eight
2. idea
3. strange
4. regular
5. swerve
6. elevator

1. ago
2. using
3. full
4. bear
5. giant
6. father

1. flood
2. blood
3. own
4. grown
5. logs
6. frogs

Boring Bill
Part Five

Bill had a new job at the Sleep More Clinic, and Bill was the star sleep maker. He would work with people who couldn't sleep. After he talked to them for a few minutes, they were making **Z**s with big smiles on their faces.

Bill was a star at making people sleep, but he still had problems. One day, he started talking to people in the elevator. When he got off the elevator, everybody else was asleep. One time after work, he started talking to the bus driver as the bus moved along the street. Soon the bus started to swerve. The driver was asleep. Bill woke up the driver just in time.

Bill kept reading books about how to be
interesting, and Bill kept trying different things. At last,
he found something that worked. He talked in a high
voice and talked faster. Nobody fell asleep. He could
talk to the people in the elevator, and they wouldn't
fall asleep. He could talk to bus drivers without putting
them to sleep.

But Bill's high voice did not work with his patients. When he talked to them in his high voice, they just looked at him and said, "This is not working. I am still awake."

So now Bill talks with two different voices. He talks in his regular, low, slower voice when he is working with patients. But when he is not helping patients sleep, he speaks in a quick, high voice. That voice sounds a little strange, but it doesn't put Milly, his friends, or doctors at the clinic to sleep. In fact, Bill is pretty popular, and people no longer call him Boring Bill. They call him the Sleep Master.

The end.

1. On line 1, write about what the tall girl fished in.

2. On line 2, write about which girl fished in a river.

A moose was bothered because he had a bug on his back. That bug kept biting him. He tried many ways to get rid of the bug. He rolled in dirt. He rubbed his back against trees. He dove under water. But none of the things the moose did stopped that bug from biting him.

At last the moose yelled, "I hate bugs."

A goose was walking by and heard the moose. The goose said, "I don't hate bugs. I love them. Bugs are good to eat."

The goose hopped up on the moose's back and ate the bug. That made the moose happy, and that made the goose happy. After that, the moose and the goose became good friends.

1. What kept biting the moose?

2. Who loved bugs?

3. The goose felt that way because bugs are ▇▇▇▇ ▇▇▇ ▇▇▇▇.

4. What did the goose do with the biting bug?

5. After that, the goose and the moose became ▇▇▇▇.

A

1. <u>Ow</u>en
2. <u>us</u>ing
3. i<u>s</u>land
4. <u>a</u>go
5. <u>tad</u>pole
6. <u>e</u>xact

B

1. pap<u>er</u>
2. t<u>ore</u>
3. grain
4. drif<u>t</u>
5. size

C

1. father
2. full
3. thought
4. through
5. giants
6. bears

D

1. <u>good</u>bye
2. <u>bob</u>bing
3. <u>pea</u>nut
4. <u>door</u>way
5. <u>c</u>lassroom
6. <u>mess</u>ages

E

1. Fizz
2. Liz
3. frog
4. hatch
5. dam

Owen, Fizz, and Liz
Part One

A long time ago, there were two islands that were almost the same in every way. They were the same size and the same shape. Both islands had a large beach on the north end. Both had a large mountain in the middle. Both had the same hills, rivers, and the same valleys. But these islands were not in the same place. They were many, many miles apart.

Another thing that was not the same about these islands was the people who lived on them. On one island, there were ten little tiny people. These people were only about one inch tall. Some of the spiders on their island were bigger than they were. On the other island, there were three giants—two parents and their boy. The parents and their boy were almost twenty feet tall. They were so big that they could not walk through the doorway of your classroom. The doorway would have to be much wider and they would have to crawl in. And they would not be able to stand up after they got inside. These giants were so big and strong that they could pick up a full grown bear and hold it like a puppy.

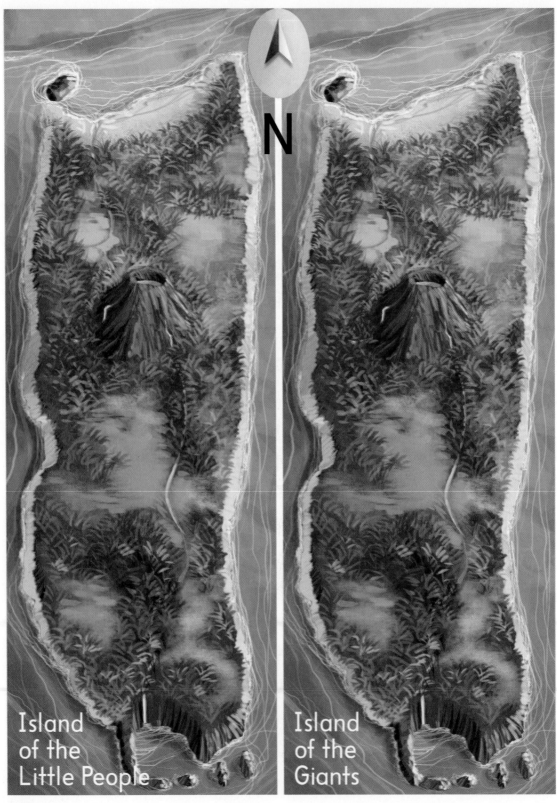

Island
of the
Little People

Island
of the
Giants

One day, one of the giants walked across the island to the big beach on the north side. As he went along the beach, he found a green bottle. To him, this bottle was very small. In fact, it was not as long as any of his fingers. The giant who found the bottle had never seen a bottle before.

The giant's name was Owen, and the only people he had ever seen were the other two giants on the island—his father and mother. Owen was almost full grown. He was about as tall as his mother, but not as tall as his father.

Owen picked up the bottle and looked at it for a long time. Then he took it home and showed it to his mother. "What is this thing?" he asked.

"That thing is a bottle," she said. Then she added, "I once heard that people can send messages to other people by using a bottle. They just write a note, put it in the bottle, close up the bottle, and put it in the water. The wind and the waves will take that bottle to another place that is far away. Somebody will find it washed up on the beach, take out the note, and read it."

More to come.

green   brown

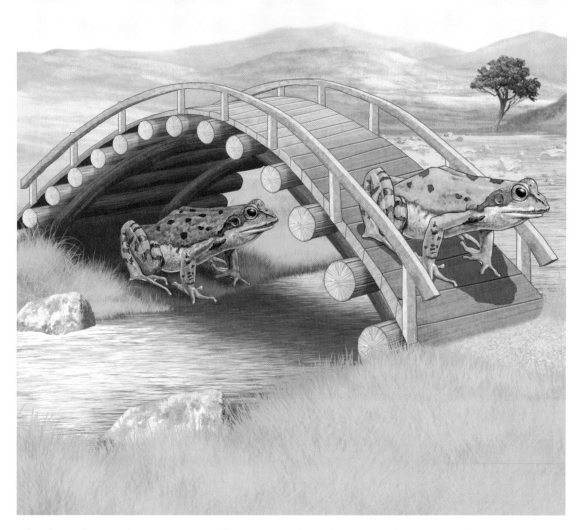

1. On line 1, write about which toad is under the bridge.

2. On line 2, write about which toad is on the bridge.

227

Bottles are made from glass. Glass is strange. When glass is very hot, it starts to get red and stops being hard. As it gets hotter, it starts to melt. At first the glass is very thick and not very soft. As the glass gets hotter, it becomes very soft and thin. It becomes like soup.

Bottles are made from this hot melted glass. The melted glass is put into a mold that is the shape of a bottle. Then air is blown inside to push the glass against the sides of the mold. When the hot glass cools, it gets hard again. The mold is opened and there is a new bottle inside.

1. What are bottles made from?
2. What happens to glass when it gets very hot?
3. To make a bottle, hot glass is put into a ▬▬▬.
4. What is blown inside to push the glass against the mold?
5. When the glass cools, what is left inside the mold?

1. <u>si</u>gnal
2. <u>dr</u>if<u>t</u>ed
3. tad<u>pole</u>
4. <u>bee</u>tle
5. pea<u>nut</u>
6. <u>p</u>ad<u>d</u>le

1. tore
2. shells
3. write
4. wrote
5. burnt
6. chart

1. tru<u>e</u>
2. watched
3. logs
4. sure
5. longer

1. re<u>tur</u>ned
2. <u>ea</u>gles
3. gr<u>ai</u>ns
4. pap<u>er</u>

1. hard-to-see
2. easy-to-see
3. imagine
4. beautiful
5. bobbing
6. fashion

229

Owen, Fizz, and Liz

Part Two

A giant named Owen found a little green bottle. He wanted to keep it, but then he started to think about what his mother had told him.

At last, he said to himself, "I think I will send a note to somebody." So he got some paper and tore off a tiny corner. Then he wrote a note in very small letters on the paper.

When Owen was done, his note said this.

Hello.

My name is Owen, and I live on a very small island. There are many small animals on this island. We have tiny tigers and tiny eagles. We also have other birds that are very tiny. Our bugs are so tiny that you can hardly see them. Please write to me if you get this note.

Owen put the note in the bottle, closed the bottle up, and put it in the water. Slowly, the bottle moved out to sea—farther and farther until Owen couldn't see it any longer. That bottle drifted and drifted away from Owen's island for three days. At last, it came to the island where the little people lived.

Two of these people were on the beach. They were named Fizz and Liz. They were not full grown, so they were not even one inch tall yet.

Fizz and Liz were throwing grains of sand into the water. For them, a grain of sand was the size of a big stone. As they played, they looked around from time to time. They wanted to make sure there were no spiders around.

Suddenly, Liz spotted the bottle bobbing in the water. She said, "Look, there's a giant green thing floating out there."

"Let's see what it is," Fizz said. So Fizz and Liz got in their racing boats. They were really peanut shells, and they were just the right size for one person to sit in and paddle around.

Fizz and Liz paddled out to the giant bottle. "There's something inside," Liz said. "Let's take this thing to shore and see what is inside."

More next time.

232

short

1. On line 1, write about what the girl with long hair ate.

2. On line 2, write about which girl ate an apple.

A boy named Ted liked to think about things. He thought about what made rain fall. He thought about why things roll down hill. One day, his dad told him, "There's a stream that is two miles from here. And that stream is moving very fast."

Ted thought about what his father told him. Then on the next day, he went to see the stream. The water was rolling down the hill and over rocks very quickly. He watched the stream on the following day and the day after that. When he returned home later that day, he told his father, "Dad, you are wrong. That stream is not moving very fast. It was in the same place every time I went to see it."

1. What did Ted like to do?
2. His dad told him there was a stream that was moving very ▨ .
3. Who went to see that stream?
4. Ted thought the stream wasn't moving fast because every time he saw it, it was in the ▨ ▨ .
5. What moved fast, the stream or the water in the stream?

152

1. wind
2. w_ind
3. l_ive
4. live
5. r_ead
6. read

1. <u>ex</u>act
2. <u>d</u>ifferences
3. <u>mountai</u>ns
4. <u>wa</u>ded
5. <u>p</u>addled

1. wrote
2. burnt
3. logs
4. tugged
5. rowed
6. climbed

1. un<u>roll</u>
2. <u>i</u>magine
3. beauti<u>ful</u>
4. <u>bee</u>tles
5. <u>v</u>alleys

Owen, Fizz, and Liz
Part Three

A bottle was bobbing in the water near the beach on the island of the little people. Fizz and Liz wanted to move the giant green bottle to the beach so they could see what was inside it. Fizz and Liz put the noses of their racing boats against the side of the bottle and paddled as hard as they could. When the bottle was very close to the shore, five other little people waded into the water. Together, they helped roll that bottle out of the water and onto the dry sand.

Fizz and Liz used ropes to open the bottle. Then four little people climbed into the bottle and tugged at the note to pull it out. It was hard work, but after a long time, they were able to pull the note out and unroll it. Liz said, "That note is as big as my front yard."

After Fizz and Liz read the note, they thought about Owen's island. Fizz said, "That place sounds very strange."

The little people didn't know that Owen's island looked the same as their island. They didn't know that the bugs, bears, birds, mountains, valleys, and rivers on Owen's island were the same size as those things on their island. The little people didn't know that Owen was so big that he could hold all of the little people in one hand.

Liz said, "Can you imagine a place with tiny birds?"

"No," Fizz said. "All our birds are bigger than a house."

Later that evening, Liz said, "Why don't we write to Owen and tell him about our island?"

So that's what they did. They turned Owen's letter over and made their note on the back. Turning the paper over was a big job. They wrote letters that were the same size as the letters Owen made. Fizz and Liz made those letters with a burnt log.

Here is their note.

Dear Owen,

Our names are Fizz and Liz, and we live on a beautiful island. It is very big, and it has big animals on it. We have big bears and big birds and big bugs. All the bugs on our island are easy to see because they are so big. Some beetles are bigger than we are.

The other little people helped roll the note up
and put it in the bottle. Then they closed up the bottle
and put the bottle in the sea. Everybody watched it
drift slowly away from their island.

More to come.

sleeping

1. On line 1, write about what the dog under the table is doing.

2. On line 2, write about where the dog is that is eating a bone.

Here are some things you may not know about peanuts. Another name for a peanut is a goober. Peanuts are also called goober peas. You read about Goober.

Here's something you may not know about peanuts. Peanuts are not really nuts. Real nuts grow above ground on nut trees. Peanuts do not grow on trees. Peanuts grow under ground. Peanuts grow on the roots of peanut plants. Peanuts are called nuts because they have shells that make them look like real nuts. Many kinds of beans are in the same plant family as peanuts.

1. What's another name for peanuts?

2. Are peanuts real nuts?

3. Do peanuts grow above ground or below ground?

4. Peanuts are in the same plant family as ▓▓▓▓ .

153

BAIT SHOP

1. <u>our</u>selves
2. <u>grass</u>hoppers
3. <u>water</u>fall
4. <u>camp</u>ground
5. <u>sun</u>light

1. l<u>i</u>ve
2. l<u>i</u>ve
3. r<u>ea</u>d
4. r<u>ea</u>d
5. w<u>i</u>nd
6. w<u>i</u>nd

1. <u>si</u>lence
2. <u>prac</u>ticed
3. <u>squeak</u>ing
4. <u>rock</u>ing
5. <u>row</u>ing
6. <u>wav</u>ing

1. ditch
2. bye
3. true
4. beautiful
5. toward
6. steal

Owen, Fizz, and Liz
Part Four

Fizz and Liz sent the green bottle, with their letter inside, out to sea. The wind and waves took the bottle back toward Owen's island. Three days after Fizz and Liz sent their note, Owen saw the bottle bobbing up and down in the water. He waded out and picked it up. When he pulled out the note, he said, "Oh, no. That's the same note I sent out."

But just as he was getting ready to throw the note away, he noticed that there was a note on the back. He read it. Then he ran back to his house and read the letter to his mom and dad.

Owen and his parents agreed that Fizz and Liz lived in a strange place. Owen's mom said, "I would hate to live in a place with bugs that were so big."

Then Owen said, "Maybe we should send another note and find out more about their island."

Owen's dad said, "Maybe we should go there and see for ourselves." Owen smiled.

"What?" Owen's mother said. "I wouldn't go to that place. I don't want to see big bugs."

Owen's dad said, "Well, let's think about it."

And they did.

One week later, Owen and his dad said that they wanted to go to the other island. It took two more weeks before Owen's mom agreed to go.

Their plan was to put the bottle in the water and let it drift. Owen and his parents would follow the bottle in their boat. Owen's family was not sure how long the trip would take, so they loaded their boat with lots of water and food.

As the sun was coming up in the morning, they put the bottle in the water and then followed it in their boat.

That is our island.

For two days, they were out in the boat with nothing around but water and the bottle. They did not see any land. Owen's family was getting very tired of sitting in the boat and rocking and bobbing with the waves. But on the third day, they spotted land.

Owen's dad started to row toward it. As they came closer and closer to the island, he stopped rowing and said, "Oh, no. That is our island. We must have just drifted out and come back to the place where we started." But he was wrong.

They rowed to the shore and pulled the boat out of the water. Owen's dad said, "Well, let's go home. I'm tired."

More next time.

1. On line 1, write about what the tall doctor is drinking from.

2. On line 2, write about which doctor is drinking from a bottle.

Things drift in water because the water moves. If you look at a river or a stream, you can see the water moving. If you throw a stick in a stream, you can see it move. The water will carry it. When a stream moves, the water is always going down hill. If the water is going down a steep hill, the water moves very fast. If the water is going down ground that is not steep, the water does not move as fast. If the water goes down a hill that is almost as steep as a wall, the water falls through the air. That's called a waterfall.

1. Things drift in water because the water ▬▬▬.
2. If you throw a stick in a stream, will it move?
3. Does the water in a stream move up hill or down hill?
4. Streams go faster when the hill is ▬▬▬.
5. When water goes down a hill almost as steep as a wall, it's called a ▬▬▬.

154

1. <u>wav</u>ing
2. <u>water</u>fall
3. <u>grass</u>hoppers
4. <u>loud</u>ly
5. <u>sudden</u>ly
6. <u>quick</u>ly

1. flood
2. area
3. idea
4. heavy
5. closely
6. build
7. eight

1. spot
2. ditch
3. speck
4. plink
5. dam
6. scratched
7. spoil

Owen, Fizz, and Liz
Part Five

Owen's family thought that they had come back to their island. They pulled their boat up on the beach and were on their way to their house.

At the same time, Fizz and Liz and five other little people were working on a barn for their turtles and grasshoppers. The turtles could pull loads that were very heavy to the little people. Grasshoppers helped the little people get from place to place quickly. The little people rode their grasshoppers like we would ride horses.

Owen's family walked to the spot on the island where their house should be, but it wasn't there. "What happened to our house?" his mother cried.

Owen's dad stared at the place their house should be with his mouth wide open.

Owen thought and rubbed his chin. Then he said, "Maybe we are not on our island."

Suddenly, Owen noticed something small that was right where his family's house would be. It was a tiny barn with only two walls and no roof. When Owen bent down and looked more closely, he saw something else—tiny, tiny people. Two of these people were waving their tiny arms and making funny squeaking sounds.

Those two people were Fizz and Liz. Fizz and Liz knew that one of the giants was Owen because his name was on his shirt. Fizz and Liz were shouting as loudly as they could. Those shouts sounded like funny squeaking sounds to the giants.

Owen bent down lower and put his ear right next to them. Then he could hear them saying, "Owen, it is Fizz and Liz."

Owen laughed. The wind from his laugh sent Fizz and Liz sailing into the grass.

We'll make a pond near the farm.

Now the giants knew why Fizz and Liz talked about bugs that were as big as they were and other large animals. And Fizz and Liz knew why Owen thought there were tiny bears, tigers, birds, and bugs on his island.

Owen, his family, and the little people went to the beach where the giants could lie down on the sand. The little people went close to the giants' ears and talked to them. Of course, the little people almost had to yell to be heard. Owen and his family could not talk very loudly, or they would blow the little people around the beach. The giants and the little people talked and talked for hours.

The next day, Owen and his family helped the little people make things. They got sticks and helped finish the barn. Then the giants dug a ditch from the waterfall to the farm to bring clean water to it. When the work was finished, the little people had clean water, a nice pond, and a park next to the farm. After working hard all day, everybody had a meal together and then went to sleep.

More to come.

cave	brown

1. On line I, write about what the black bear lived in.

2. On line 2, write about which bear lived in a tree.

Toads and Frogs

Toads and frogs lay eggs. When toads and frogs first hatch from their eggs, they are called tadpoles. Tadpoles live in water and don't need air. They look more like fish than frogs or toads. They have a long tail for swimming, but they do not have legs.

Then tadpoles start to change. Their long tails become shorter, and legs start to grow. When tadpoles are done changing into frogs or toads, they can not live under water any more because they need air. But frogs and toads can go a long time under water and are very good swimmers.

Frogs and toads eat a lot of bugs. So farmers like to have frogs and toads around their ponds. Many of the bugs that frogs and toads eat are bugs that bite people or eat plants the farmer grows for people to eat.

1. What are frogs and toads first called when they hatch?

2. Those things live in ▮▮▮▮ .

3. When frogs and toads are done changing, can they live under water?

4. What do frogs eat?

5. Who likes to have frogs and toads around their ponds?

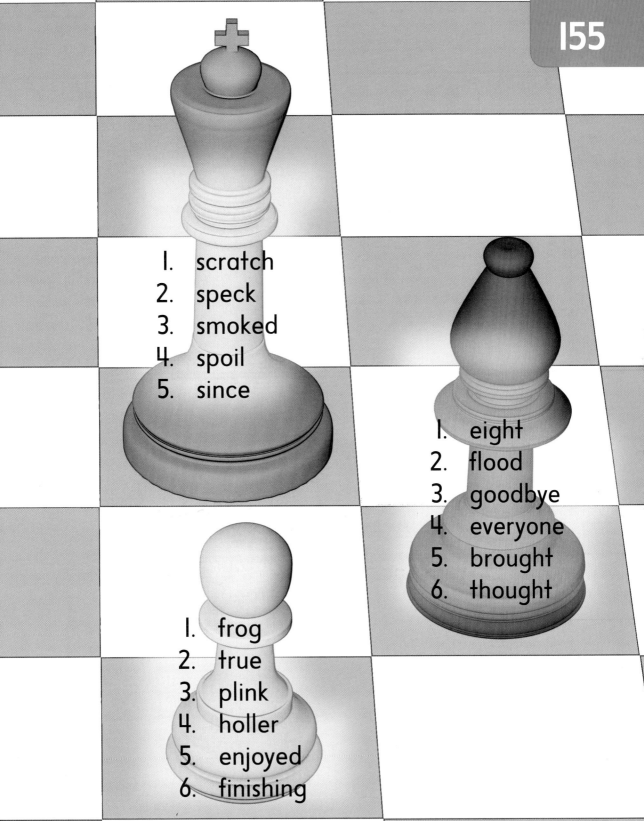

155

1. scratch
2. speck
3. smoked
4. spoil
5. since

1. eight
2. flood
3. goodbye
4. everyone
5. brought
6. thought

1. frog
2. true
3. plink
4. holler
5. enjoyed
6. finishing

Owen, Fizz, and Liz
Part Six

Owen and his family stayed with the little people for three days. In that time, Owen's family did more work for the little people than the little people could have done in two years. The little people had eight new houses and a beautiful campground near the mountains. They had a large storeroom for keeping food like fish. And they had lots and lots of fish.

Owen and his family had gone fishing and brought back more fish than the little people had ever seen in one place before. The little people salted and smoked these fish so they wouldn't spoil. Then Owen's mom worked with the little people to put the smoked fish in the storeroom.

258

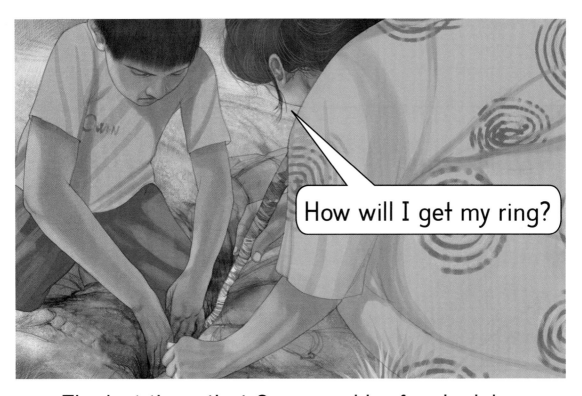

How will I get my ring?

The last thing that Owen and his family did was build a dam between the waterfall and the pond they had made. The dam would make sure that the pond would not flood in the spring. Owen and his family had to go part way up the mountain to get rocks for the dam. As Owen's mother was lifting a rock, it slipped. As the rock fell, it pulled her gold ring off of her finger.

Plink. The ring fell in a crack between very large rocks. The giants could not reach the ring with their hands or with a stick. As strong as the giants were, they could not move the rocks to get the ring either. "This is awful," Owen's mom said. "I can't leave without my beautiful ring."

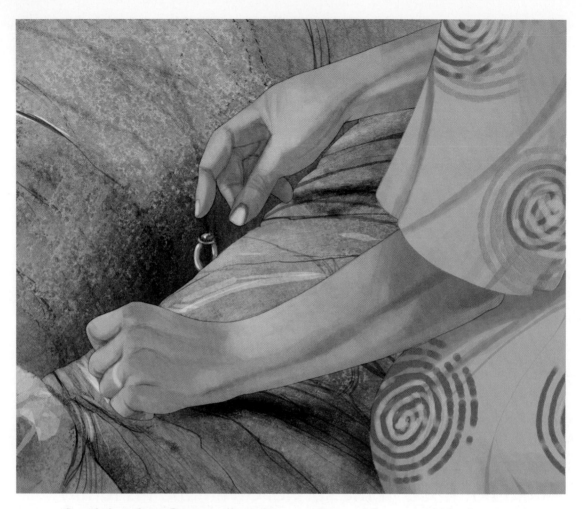

Suddenly, Owen had an idea. He raced down to where the little people were. He picked up Fizz and Liz and raced back. He showed them where the ring was and asked them, "Do you think you could go down there and get the ring?"

"That would be easy," Fizz and Liz said. And it was. In no time, Fizz and Liz crawled into the crack and went under the ring. Together, Fizz and Liz lifted the ring up so that Owen's mom could grab it.

"Oh, thank you," Owen's mom said.

After finishing the dam and visiting with the little people one more evening, it was time for Owen and his family to go home. In the morning, when Owen's family was ready to leave, Owen's dad took the green bottle out to the beach and put it in the water. As the little people watched on the beach, Owen's family pushed their boat into the water, jumped in, and said goodbye to the little people. The little people waved and shouted. Everyone had tears in their eyes. The little people stood there and watched the boat and the bottle move farther and farther out to sea. As the boat drifted out of sight, the little people could see the giants waving and hear the giants shouting to them. "So long my friends. Remember to come visit us some time soon."

Finally, the boat of the giants was only a speck way out in the sea. Fizz and Liz said, "Some day, we will visit Owen's island and see our friends again."

The end.

1. On line I, write about where the brown car went.

2. On line 2, write about the car that went down the hill.

Differences Between Frogs and Toads

You can see the difference between frog tadpoles and toad tadpoles. Toad tadpoles are darker. Toad tadpoles take longer to grow up.

Full grown toads have big bumps on their skin. Most frogs have smooth skin. Toads don't have teeth, but frogs have teeth. Frogs have bigger back legs, so they are able to move more quickly and jump farther.

Frogs and toads eat the same kinds of food. But most frogs hunt for their food when it is day time. Most toads hide while the sun is out and hunt for food at night.

1. Which are darker, toad or frog tadpoles?

2. Which tadpoles grow up faster?

3. What do toads have on their skin that frogs do not have?

4. Frogs have bigger ____.

5. What time of day do most toads hunt for food?

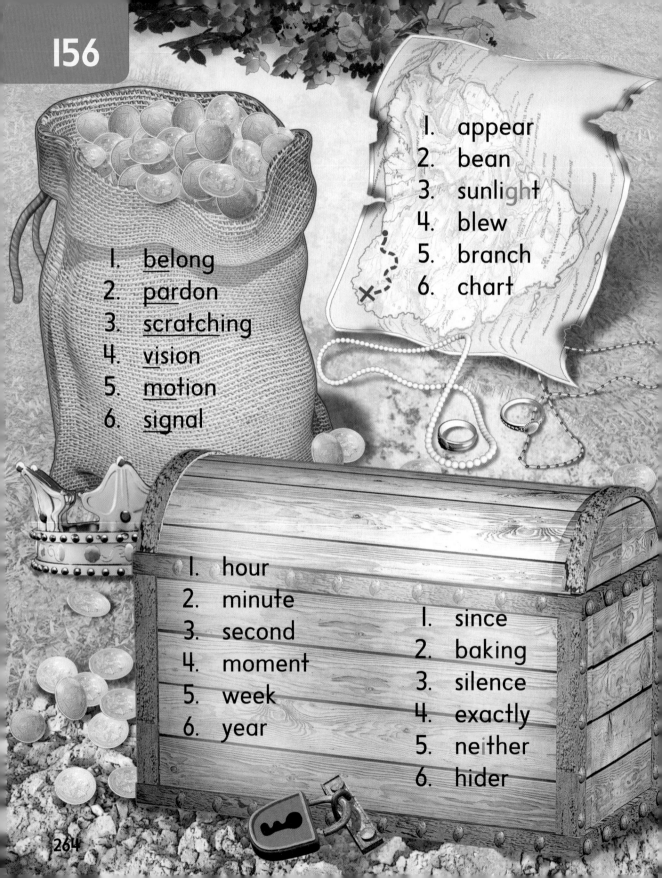

156

1. <u>be</u>long
2. <u>par</u>don
3. <u>scr</u>atching
4. <u>v</u>ision
5. <u>mo</u>tion
6. <u>s</u>ignal

1. appear
2. bean
3. sunlight
4. blew
5. branch
6. chart

1. hour
2. minute
3. second
4. moment
5. week
6. year

1. since
2. baking
3. silence
4. exactly
5. neither
6. hider

The Hiding Contest
Part One

A few weeks after the circus, the bragging rats started arguing again. The other rats in the pack were tired of listening to their noisy arguments. They went to the wise old rat and once again said, "We must do something to make Moe and Sherlock shut up. Help us out."

The wise old rat thought for a few minutes and then said, "I think I have a plan for another contest. That contest will fool the bragging rats into being quiet for a long time."

The wise old rat went over to where Moe and Sherlock were arguing, and he asked, "Which of you rats is the best at hiding?"

Sherlock spoke first. He said that he could hide in the middle of a street in bright sunlight without anyone seeing him.

Moe spoke next. He said, "I am such an expert at hiding that I could be right next to you and you would not be able to see me."

"Stop," the wise old rat said. "There is only one way to settle this argument."

You know how they settled it. They had a hiding contest. The wise old rat told Sherlock and Moe, "You go hide, and after a while, we'll come looking for you. The first one we find is the loser of the contest. The loser must not brag about hiding ever again."

The bragging rats went and hid. The wise old rat said to the others, "Now we will have peace for a while. In three hours, we will go looking for them."

One of the other rats said, "I can see them now. Moe is right over there near those weeds, and Sherlock is behind that tree."

The wise old rat said, "I know. But let's enjoy the quiet for a few hours." And that's just what the other rats did. They read and whispered and just enjoyed the peace and quiet.

To make sure the bragging rats wanted to keep hiding, every once in a while, one of the rat pack would walk by a bragging rat and say something like, "Where are Moe and Sherlock? We are looking for them everywhere. We can't find them anywhere. They must be experts at hiding."

The time passed pretty slowly for Sherlock and Moe. But for the other rats in the pack, the time seemed to fly by quickly. And before they knew it, three hours had passed.

More next time.

1. On line 1, write what the girl is reading about.

2. On line 2, write what the boy is reading about.

There was a baby mouse who loved to bounce her tiny ball. The mouse bounced that ball day and night. One morning, the baby mouse was bouncing the ball outside her mouse hole, and a cat saw her. That cat whispered to himself, "I will pounce on that mouse."

But just as the cat started to pounce, the mouse bounced the tiny ball so it went right in the cat's nose. That ball got stuck way up the cat's nose. The ball going up his nose shocked him so much that he missed the baby mouse. The cat shook his head and blew air out of his nose to free the ball. But the ball stayed in the cat's nose. Finally, the cat sneezed, but the ball did not come out.

The mother mouse came out and said, "Ho, ho, Mister Cat. You don't have a mouse in your mouth. You have a ball up your nose."

The ball stayed in the cat's nose for a few hours before it came out. The cat didn't pounce on mice after that.

1. Who loved to bounce her ball?

2. The baby mouse bounced the ball day and ▬▬▬ .

3. Who was the cat going to pounce on?

4. The ball got stuck in the cat's ▬▬▬ .

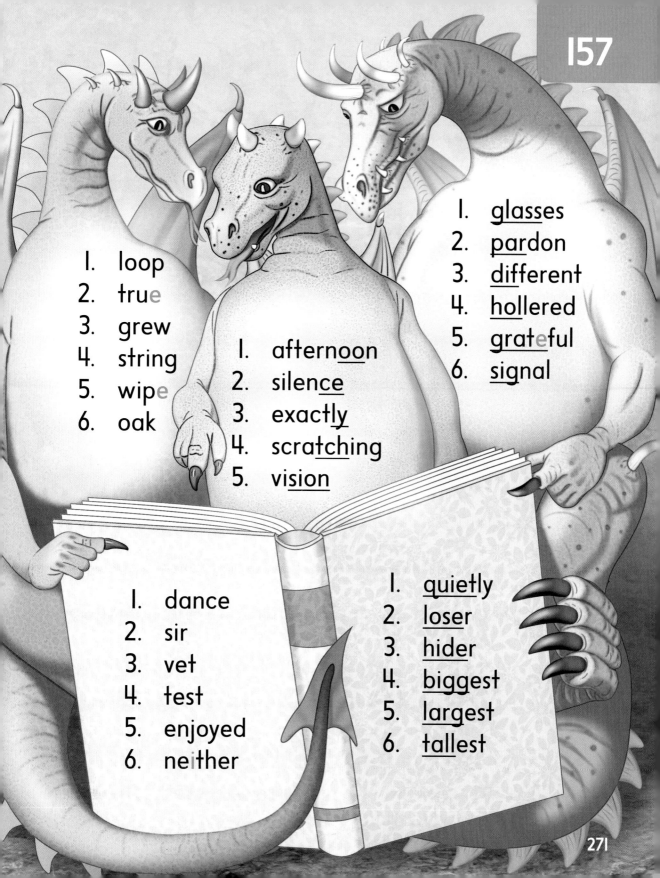

157

1. loop
2. true
3. grew
4. string
5. wipe
6. oak

1. afternoon
2. silence
3. exactly
4. scratching
5. vision

1. glasses
2. pardon
3. different
4. hollered
5. grateful
6. signal

1. dance
2. sir
3. vet
4. test
5. enjoyed
6. neither

1. quietly
2. loser
3. hider
4. biggest
5. largest
6. tallest

The Hiding Contest
Part Two

The rat pack enjoyed three hours of silence as the bragging rats hid. At last, the wise old rat quietly told the others, "It's time to find Moe and Sherlock. We must find them at exactly the same time." The wise old rat continued, "If we find them at different times, one of the bragging rats will win and one of them will lose. Then, the hiding contest will be over."

None of the rat pack wanted that. So some of the rats went over to where Sherlock was behind the tree. He was easy to see because he was scratching and talking to himself. The other rats went over to where Moe was. He was trying to hide behind some weeds in the field, but two crows were right next to him asking what he was doing. When the wise old rat gave the signal, some of the rats went up to Sherlock and shouted, "We found you!" At the same time, the other rats in the rat pack moved closer to Moe and yelled, "We found you!"

The wise old rat explained to Sherlock and Moe, "We found both of you at exactly the same time, so neither one of you won the contest."

Moe said, "You found Sherlock first."

Sherlock said, "No way. You found Moe first."

"Stop arguing," the wise old rat said. "We will settle this argument with another hiding contest tomorrow."

"Okay," Moe said. "But tomorrow, I'll hide so well you may never find me."

"Oh yeah?" Sherlock said. "I'm going to hide so well that your children will still be looking for me six years from now."

"Oh yeah?" Moe said. "I'll hide so well that . . . "

The pack had to listen to a lot of arguing that evening. But the next day, they put on another hiding contest. That contest was a lot like the first contest, except that the other rats waited four hours before they found the bragging rats.

And, of course, the pack found Moe and Sherlock at exactly the same time.

Do you know that those hiding contests are still going on? It's true. Whenever the pack can't stand Sherlock and Moe any longer, they ask them who is the best hider. Then the pack can get the bragging rats to have another hiding contest and shut up for the next few hours. While the bragging rats are quiet, all the other rats are very happy.

The end.

black

1. On line 1, write about what the brown haired woman washed.

2. On line 2, write about who drove a tan car.

There once was a snake that was sad. The other animals were playing kick ball. They had legs, so they could kick the ball. The snake did not have legs, so it could not kick the ball.

One day the snake said, "I think I can hit that ball with my head."

The first time the snake tried to make the ball move by hitting it with its head, the ball did not go very far. But the snake practiced and practiced. After working hard for ten weeks, the snake could hit the ball a long way and bounce the ball very quickly.

The other animals saw the snake hitting and bouncing the ball with its head and let the snake play kick ball with them. The snake won the game and all the animals were happy. All the other animals said, "That snake really knows how to use its head."

1. At first, the snake was sad because it could not kick ▊▊▊▊ .

2. The snake couldn't kick the ball because it didn't have ▊▊▊▊ .

3. What did the snake practice hitting the ball with?

4. Did the other animals let the snake play ball?

5. The other animals said, "That snake can really use its ▊▊▊▊ ."

158

1. vet
2. oak
3. test
4. scream
5. trash
6. h<u>ow</u>ling

1. s<u>ir</u>
2. <u>ch</u>art
3. vi<u>sion</u>
4. tr<u>ea</u>t
5. c<u>ou</u>ch

1. knocked
2. head
3. heavy
4. warm
5. shoe

1. <u>grate</u>ful
2. <u>after</u>noon
3. <u>glass</u>es
4. <u>holl</u>ering
5. <u>par</u>don
6. <u>hund</u>reds

1. lose
2. use
3. gather
4. rather
5. might
6. sight

277

Gorman Gets Glasses

One day, Gorman came into the barn and ran into a pile of pots for growing plants. Gorman said, "Pardon me, sir. I didn't see you standing there."

Clarabelle said to Gorman, "There isn't a man here. You're speaking to the pile of pots you just knocked over."

Gorman laughed and said, "I was just making a joke."

"No," Clarabelle said. "Your vision is really bad. You need glasses."

Clarabelle told Gorman that the vet was coming to the farm that day. She was sure that the vet could make glasses so he could see better.

So that afternoon, the vet gave Gorman an eye test. She set a chart on a tall oak tree. There were letters on that chart. Gorman stood ten yards from the chart. The vet told him, "Read all the letters. Start with the biggest letter at the top of the chart."

Gorman asked, "What chart?"

The vet said, "The chart on the oak tree."

Gorman asked, "What oak tree?"

The vet said, "My, my. This goat's vision is not good. He really needs strong glasses."

The vet told Gorman to stand closer and closer to the chart. With each step closer, Gorman still couldn't see. Finally, he was only one foot from the chart, and he could read the big letter **E** at the top. After the test with the chart, the vet looked in Gorman's eyes and did some other tests.

Finally, the vet said, "I will have glasses for you two weeks from now. The glasses will be very thick and heavy, but your sight will be much better."

Who is that silly looking animal?

Two weeks later, when the vet returned, she tested Gorman's vision with his new glasses. The vet put the eye chart on the oak tree. She had Gorman stand next to Clarabelle, ten yards in front of the chart. The vet told Gorman to keep his eyes closed as she tied the new glasses around his head. Then she said, "Open your eyes and tell me what you see."

Gorman looked around. He looked left. He looked right. Suddenly, Gorman jumped. "Help," he hollered. "What is that great brown and white thing next to me?"

Clarabelle said, "Gorman, it's me, your friend Clarabelle."

When Gorman was no longer in shock, the vet tested him on the letter chart. Gorman was able to name all the letters on the eye chart. He did very well on all of the other eye tests too.

Gorman wanted to be alone so he went to the pond and looked at himself in the water. "Who is that silly looking animal?" he asked.

As Gorman stared at himself, his glasses slipped off and fell into the water. Gorman said. "Oh, no. Without my glasses, I will never find my glasses."

A voice said, "Don't say never." Then the voice said, "Brothers, sisters, and pals, let's see who can find those glasses first."

Within seconds, many toads jumped from the shore into the pond to look for Gorman's glasses. The toads found Gorman's glasses right away. The toads returned the glasses and, of course, Gorman was very grateful.

After Gorman put on his glasses, he said to the leader toad, "You are a strange looking animal, but I would like to be your friend." And that's just what happened. From that day on, Gorman and the leader toad were good friends.

The end.

brown	plate

1. On line 1, write about what the white dog is eating from.

2. On line 2, write about which dog is drinking from a cup.

Once there was a tom cat that lived in the city, but he didn't have a home. One night was very cold. All the other street cats were complaining because they didn't have anything warm to sleep on. The tom cat said, "I'll show you how to get some warm things to sleep on."

He got up on a fence and started to howl very loudly. "Meoooooowwwww," he howled.

Some other cats joined in and started howling too. Within a few seconds, people started to throw things at the cats. Somebody threw a big shoe. Somebody else threw an old rug. Somebody else threw a coat with a hole in it.

The tom cat said, "Now we have lots of good things to sleep on."

The cats made a pile out of the warm things. That night got very cold, but the cats stayed warm and had a good sleep with a rug and coat around them.

1. Did the tom cat have a home?

2. Was the night cold?

3. What did the tom cat do to get people to throw things at him?

4. Write two of the things that people threw at the cats.

5. Were the cats cold that night?

159

1. oil
2. choose
3. hottest
4. eaten
5. minutes

1. Scoville
2. tongue
3. omnivores
4. pictures
5. areas

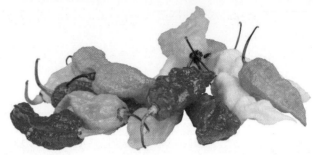

Hot Peppers

The peppers from some pepper plants are crisp and taste sweet. Many kinds of peppers have a hot taste when you bite into them. Hot peppers do not feel warm if you hold them in your hand. But if someone bites into a hot pepper, it can make the person feel like their mouth is on fire.

Milk and food made from milk, like cheese, cream, and butter, can take the burn from hot peppers away. Another way of making the burning go away is time.

If your mouth burns really badly from eating hot peppers, it may take a long time—many minutes or even hours—before the burning feeling goes away.

One of the scales that tells how hot peppers are is called the Scoville scale. Bell peppers are not hot at all. You can eat bell peppers without making your mouth burn. Below are pictures of bell peppers. You can see that the mark for the heat score of bell peppers on the Scoville scale is zero.

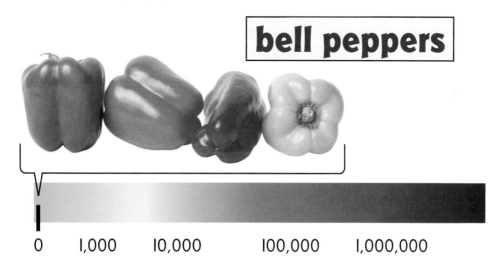

Some chili peppers are not very hot, some are hot, and some can be really hot. Below is a picture of a chili pepper. You can see that the mark for the heat score of a chili pepper on the Scoville scale is 10,000.

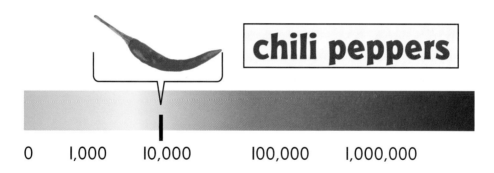

Almost everybody can hold very hot peppers in their hands because the skin of your hands is thick. The oil from the hot peppers does not get through that thick skin. But oil that gets on a person's hand can rub off on their face and other areas with thin skin. On areas with thin skin, the oil will feel like it is burning. If people get hot pepper oil on their cheeks and chin, it will burn and make that skin red. If people get the hot pepper oil in their eyes, it will make their eyes water and they may start to cry. It is a good idea to wash your hands very well after you touch hot peppers.

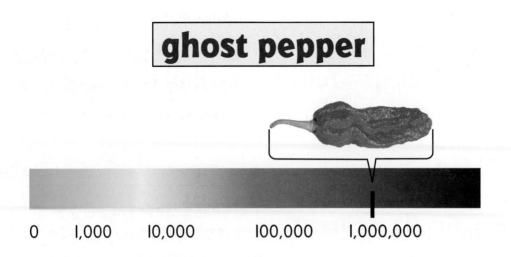

ghost pepper

0   1,000   10,000   100,000   1,000,000

People who are not used to eating hot peppers and take a few bites of a really hot pepper may get sores on their lips and tongue. If someone eats too many of those peppers, they can also get sick.

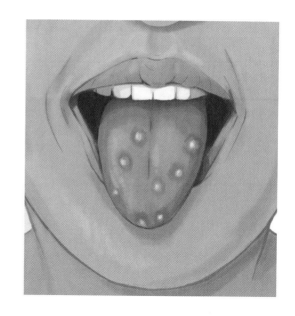

People who grow up eating hot peppers don't get sores on the inside of their mouths from eating them. These people often like the taste and feeling from eating hot peppers.

Many animals will eat peppers that are not hot and sometimes peppers that are hot. Hot peppers will do the same things to most mammals that they do to people.

What Animals Eat

Some animals eat only grass or other foods from plants like nuts, peppers, corn, leaves, apples, peas, and beans.

Many animals eat foods that come from other animals. There are two kinds of foods from other animals. One kind of food is the meat from the body of animals like steak and hamburger. The other kind is food that comes from things that animals make like eggs, milk, and honey. Some of the foods that people make out of the milk from cows and goats are cheese, butter, and cream.

Animals that eat both foods from plants and foods from animals are called omnivores. People are omnivores. All people can live on meat and food from animals, but some people choose not to eat meat. Some of these people also choose not to eat any food that comes from animals.

Some birds eat seeds and plants. A snow goose is a bird that eats only food from plants.

Crows and black birds are omnivores. If there is meat or eggs for them to eat, they will eat that food. Black birds and crows will also eat nuts and other food from plants.

Some birds eat other animals. Hawks and eagles are birds that eat only meat from other animals.

Mammals like cows, goats, moose, sheep, and horses never eat meat, but they drink their mother's milk when they are babies. When those mammals grow up, they eat only plants.

Mammals chew their food, so when they eat parts of plants with seeds, they kill the seeds. Some pepper plants became hot to try to keep mammals from eating them and killing their seeds. The oil from hot pepper plants fools mammals into feeling like the peppers are burning their mouth. Most mammals will stay away from hot pepper plants because it hurts to eat hot peppers. Many people know that food made from milk can take the burn from hot peppers away.

Birds do not chew when they eat seeds, so they do not kill seeds. Birds help plants because they drop live seeds that they have eaten wherever they go. Dropping these seeds gives those plants more chances to live and grow. Since birds help plants, birds do not feel pain from the oil that makes hot peppers painful to most mammals.

Some beetles and some turtles are omnivores. Dogs, rats, mice, and pigs are mammals that are omnivores. Pigs are farm animals that like to eat anything you like to eat.

Pigs really likes burgers and fries, apples and corn. Pigs also like a lot of foods you wouldn't eat. Pigs like rotten food and scraps that people throw away.

Pigs can eat almost everything.

PHOTO CREDITS